From Relationsh*t
to Relationship

Quantity discounts are available on bulk orders.
Contact sales@TAGPublishers.com for more information.

TAG Publishing, LLC
2618 S. Lipscomb
Amarillo, TX 79109
www.TAGPublishers.com

Office (806) 373-0114
Fax (806) 373-4004
info@TAGPublishers.com

ISBN: 978-1-59930-398-7

First Edition

Text: Lloyd Arbour, www.tablloyd.com

From Relationsh*t
to Relationship

Ossi and Dan Graicer

TABLE OF CONTENTS

INTRODUCTION

You've made a commitment to join in marriage with a very special someone. Or perhaps you've been married for several years. Either way, congratulations! Marriage can be trying even under the best of circumstances. Often times a relationship can turn into a relationshit. One moment you may want to shower your partner with flowers and affection and the next you wonder what demon spirit possessed you to marry such a person. Something you may realize already is that strong, healthy, long-lasting marriages don't just happen on their own. They happen when two people are intentional in their dreams, desires, and commitment.

The days of a young bride in a white wedding gown are in the past. Marriages happen in different ways and at different times for different people. You may be young, middle-aged, older, or on your first, second, or even third marriage (if that's the case then you really need our book). You may get married in a home, a church, a synagogue, a temple, or a courthouse. None of this really matters. All that is important in a marriage is that there is a relationship of love based on:

- Communication
- Trust

- Cooperation
- Intimacy
- Mutual respect

While no two marriages look exactly alike, all people enter marriage with similar hopes. Happy, loving, forever. We don't ever want to lose that initial attraction and passion. But what happens six months down the road when the husband has to take a break from shaving to toss his wife some toilet paper? There's been a good deal of research conducted about the kinds of behaviors that people do that lead to strong, long-lasting marriages. *From Relationsh*t to Relationship* is designed to share the many life lessons we have learned as well as some helpful information with you about conflict, communication, and changing your thought process. Some of this might confirm what you're doing already; some of this might be new, and some might make you think we're nuts. As they say, the proof is in the pudding or, in our case, the wedding cake. We've been married for thirty years and have seen our share of trials and tribulations and have even played catch with a roll of toilet paper a time or two. Our goal is to help you learn how to build a successful marriage with your best friend, lover, and partner for life. In a time of constant debate about the meaning of commitment and forever, we want to show you how to build a vision of taking care of each other as you grow older and of being there for each other through life's ups and downs.

We hope that both you and your spouse will benefit from our experience. As daily physical exercise builds strong bodies, relationship exercises build strong marriages. In each chapter, we've included various exercises and tips to help foster your own happy marriage. Work through these exercises with your partner as you read and try out some of the tips in the weeks, months, and years ahead. Just as marriage is forever, so is this book. Save it and refer back to it on a frequent basis, especially when questions or difficult situations arise in your relationship. Each chapter teaches valuable tips, skills, and thoughts that form the foundation for solid marriages for both men and women.

Healthy marriages create happy communities—something we all want. Let us help you and your efforts to build a strong and lasting marriage. We wish you all the best in creating the life you and your partner have always dreamed of.

CHAPTER 1
I DID, BUT NOW I'M NOT SURE WHY

*"All marriages are happy. It's living
together afterwards that is difficult."*

–UNKNOWN

CHAPTER 1

Our paradigms (habits) determine who we are and what type of marriage we'll have. They guide us throughout our lives, influencing our decisions and actions. Creating a paradigm shift is the key to creating our ideal marriage. Everything we perceive in our marriage world has its origin in the invisible, inner world of our thoughts and beliefs. To become the master of our destiny, we must learn to control the nature of our dominant, habitual thoughts. We need to make the decision to find our own beliefs and stop letting our paradigms control our actions and behaviors. Once we're able to do so, we'll move from confusion to order, release any past hurts, and move forward to a successful and happy marriage.

The state of mind of the majority of couples we work with is mass confusion. They know they're not happy and that there are issues, but they honestly don't know what caused and in most cases is still causing their problems. Imagine a sleep walker. They get up in the middle of the night and wander around the house only to find themselves waking up on the kitchen table the next morning. They have no idea how they got there because they can't remember getting up in the middle of the night. This is the type of confusion most marriages face today.

We're sure that at some time or another, almost all married people find themselves confronting confusion. During these times, they have reached a low point in their relationship where they feel at a loss for what to do. In most cases, these thoughts are transient and disappear once the issues causing the stress and confusion reside. These feelings, however, are just like chronic headaches; they may go away temporarily, but rest assured they'll be back again in a few weeks. The good news is that there's hope. You can find order out of the confusion by changing your thinking, feelings, and behavior. (Notice we said yours, not theirs.)

HE SAID, SHE SAID

The only real life preparation for marriage we had was from the front row seat at our own parents' marriage. Have you seen a movie in a foreign language? You sit down and watch scenes and think to yourself: "I wish to hell I knew what was going on" and "Where are the subtitles?" For most of us this is how we grew up; our parents acted out their life in front of us and we had no clue what was going on because our parents never sat us down and explained the subtleties of a successful marriage. The majority of our parents didn't realize that their marriage was setting an example for their children's marriages because they didn't view marriage as something that they needed to educate us about.

Our parents are a good example of the differences in marriage. Both of our parents were Holocaust survivors. This horrendous event had an effect on their relationships. One couple lived a happy marriage and cherished each other, while the other spent their days in a dominating and volatile marriage. It was only natural that when we entered into our marriage, we expected it to be the same as our respective parents'.

"My father was overbearing and expected my mother to do what he said without question, and she did. She catered to his every need, and when he said "jump" she said "how high." Every night, he came home and dinner was ready and the house was spotless. I thought this was how my marriage was going to be too. I expected Ossi to do everything I said. Only she had a mind of her own and wanted our marriage to be equal. I didn't know any different; this was the example I had growing up in my home." Dan

When most people look at their marriage they think they know what they want, but these desires are, more often than not, based on their paradigms. A paradigm is a group of habits that you subconsciously accepted as you grew into an adult. With this definition in mind, think about your parents' marriage. Do you see any of their beliefs and habits in your current relationship? Paradigms are important for two reasons. First, these beliefs establish boundaries and limits you have placed on your life. Second, they instruct your behavior. Your parents' actions in their marriage are all you know. Everything you think about marriage is based on others, which causes confusion.

We hear so many people say, "I know what I want, but I'm not getting it." We then pose the question, "Is it really what you want or what you think you want?" Until we have a paradigm shift our wants aren't really ours. A paradigm shift occurs when a change in mindset occurs. New paradigms develop when old (or current) paradigms no longer work. In one of our seminars, we met a couple thinking about divorce. His job in construction requires him to be on the jobsite at 6 am. By the time he gets home, usually around 4 pm, he is tired and wants to sit on the couch, watch TV, and rest. His wife, on the other hand, doesn't get home until 7, and when she walks in the door and sees him sitting on the couch, she gets furious.

Our first question to her was about her father. We asked her what he was like when she was a child. Her answer instantly gave us the answer we were looking for. Her parents were divorced, and she was ashamed of her father because she has always heard her mother talk about how lazy he was. She too then accepted this belief about her father. So when she looked at her husband she saw her dad sitting on the couch, not her husband. Couples believe that arguments and disagreements stem from their spouse's actions, but in all reality they are a direct result of paradigms. How different would your marriage be if you could shift your paradigms?

Everyone's mind is controlled by patterns of thoughts representing certain beliefs. For many of you, these beliefs are self-defeating. As you mature, these childhood beliefs are the foundation for much of who you become, and they affect the way you perceive your marriage. Your personalities and identities were formed many years ago when you were a small child. Have you ever considered that some of these beliefs aren't true? That they were placed upon you at such an early age that you didn't have the ability or authority to question whether they were correct or not? So you, like millions of others, just accepted them as is. This false explanation that you tell yourself creates an unrealistic version of how your life should be, not how it actually is. You tend to focus on perceptions instead of reality. Your marriage then becomes ingrained with these perceptions.

Uncovering your paradigms is a vital part of a happy marriage. In order to uncover these beliefs we first have to find some of the origins of your past beliefs. As children, your parents or those closest to you were your entire world. From your earliest moments, any of their interactions determined what type of spouse you'd be and consequently, what kind of perceptions you would carry with you into your relationships. Did you ever feel ignored, unaccepted, unloved, or dissatisfied as a child? If any of these feelings existed inside you as a child, you instinctively tried to:

- Absolve your family member from any responsibility for the hurt because you still needed them to love and protect you.

- Search for a new way to connect to them.

These perceptions move farther away from their original source and morph into a distorted sense of reality in your marriage. It is important to uncover the source so that you can stop relying on your childlike responses and make positive, healthy, mature decisions, limiting beliefs or negative thoughts that have been repeated so much that they have now become part of your belief system. That's it! All beliefs are just thoughts you have continued to think for a very long time.

Now, some beliefs definitely serve you. You know them because every time you practice these beliefs, you feel good. But others do not make you feel good. These are called limiting beliefs. So, in knowing this, isn't it easy to entertain the idea of choosing new thoughts? In time, the new thoughts replace the old beliefs, supporting your vision for your life and who you want to be.

Paradigms exist in every aspect of our lives. They show up in conversations, books, bedrooms, families, and professions. Paradigms fall within paradigms, overlap other paradigms, and bump into others still. They are big or small, new or old, comfortable or uncomfortable, familiar or unfamiliar, long-term or short-lived. What are the paradigms in your life? Look as deeply as you wish, noticing any resistance or other feelings you experience as you respond to the following questions:

- Are the beliefs you grew up with still an integral part of your life?
- How happy is your marriage?
- When you have a disagreement with your spouse, how do you respond?
- How do you feel about change? Do you resist it?

Based on your answers, what paradigms do you wish to shift?

THINK MORE DO LESS

Thoughts control the world. Everything in the universe was once a thought. The paper this book is printed on, the computer used to create it, and all of the words inside. Our thoughts are the keys to our success. In order for you to have a fulfilling marriage, it is imperative to understand the thought process and release your paradigms. The problem is we put too much effort into changing the other person and very little into changing our own behavior. We think too little and try to do too much when all we need to do is think more and do less. You must educate yourself about the workings of the mind. This is the defining distinction between successful and unsuccessful marriages. Thoughts are very powerful and can pave your way to success or barricade you from ever achieving everlasting love. Once you unleash the power of your mind, you can use it to your advantage and obtain anything you want in life. We believe that we are nature's masterpiece of creation; therefore success is an innate aspect of our existence. We were all born to be successful, no matter what we think!

Each one of us has at least 60,000 thoughts every day. That is an astonishing figure, but even more astonishing is that the majority of these thoughts is negative and doesn't originate in your own mind. Even though you and your spouse may be living in confusion, on the edge, in the middle, over the top, spaced out, freaked out, or in the void, there are things you can do to take advantage of the circumstances. First of all, find out which paradigms are controlling your actions. This gives you the power to make a decision to change. Remember, think more and do less. Write your feelings in your life changes journal or speak privately into a tape recorder. Talk about how you feel. Tell them you're upset and what you perceive to be wrong. Stay with this process until you quiet down.

"When Dan and I would argue he would always have a way to convince me that I was wrong. I couldn't tell him my true feelings because I had dismissed them before I had a chance to voice them. So one day I decided that I would write a letter to Dan telling him exactly how I felt. This was the perfect solution because he could see my feelings through my eyes instead of through his." Ossi

Write or speak all your concerns, options, fears, and hesitancies. There is a kind of natural organizing process that happens as you put things on paper. Start by writing your most urgent questions and feelings of confusion on the left side. List what you want or how you want to feel on the right side. Visualize all the heavy feelings you are carrying in your body draining down into the earth as you write your letter or record your voice. Then once you've emptied out, think about a good quality of your spouse. Draw in that "refined" thought and release any negative emotions. Your goal is to disconnect from the negative thoughts and recenter your physical body to establish a calm, grounded feeling. Think back to a time when you felt true love. For example, a woman in one of our classes remembered a time when her husband bought her flowers just because. As she thought about her pleasant memory, she wrote down some of her feelings. Out of that memory, it occurred to her how much her husband meant to her.

This may sound like a difficult process when you're mad our upset because in the past you wouldn't dream of releasing any anger or frustration. Remember, though, you're creating a paradigm shift. Just because your father or mother held a grudge and yelled and screamed doesn't mean you have to. Something in you is changing. You are shedding old skin. You want to move forward in your marriage. If you're not moving ahead, you're going backwards. A paradigm shift can bring a new feeling into the relationship, new possibilities, no matter where you are on your journey. Anything is possible.

MAKE THE DECISION

Trust your feelings. We came to a pivotal point in our marriage when we wondered if it was worth saving. We decided to go to a marriage counselor. The problem was that in marriage counseling the therapist told us what to do. He gave us advice to do this or do that.

> *"Our marriage counseling cost us $250,000. Not in fees but in a failed business. I went with his suggestion to give Ossi some freedom and allow her to open a fashion company. A quarter of a million dollars later, we were in a worse situation. Our marriage was bad and now we were broke." Dan*

None of his advice addressed our paradigms. Advice is like a fruit basket—you may get one or two things that you like, but eventually you want something else. Have you ever stopped to wonder why so many people pray? God doesn't give advice, He just listens. People want to be heard, not told what to do. In marriage, each person needs to come to his or her own understanding of what he or she needs and wants. For us, marriage counseling was an expensive lesson because we needed to know what was happening in our own minds, not each other's.

We have often heard people in our workshops talk about how they reached the point of no return and can't let go of the hurt and anger. When we ask if there is still love, they say yes. Why is it then that we're willing to walk away and lose our marriage even though we still have an emotional connection? Simple because we can't release the past. Focus on the results you desire, the feeling of success and happiness you want. Confusion, frustration, and anger will only make things worse. If you do not deal well with this feeling things are only going to move backward.

> *"My turning point happened several years ago. I made up in my mind to get a divorce. I looked at my marriage and didn't see any future. So for the next 10 nights, I dreamed of being divorced. Each morning when I woke up and thought about how my life looked after I was divorced I didn't seem happy. To me, this meant that I had to release my feelings of hurt. For I had to assume that all my relationship models and beliefs were wrong and I needed to build new ones, so I did. From that moment our marriage started to bloom." Dan*

Although you may be harboring feelings of anger, make sure at all times that you make judgments rationally and not emotionally. Do not let your emotion take control of you and allow you to do or say things that you will regret. Never forget that a harsh word spoken cannot be reversed. The uncontrolled release of anger is a childish habit. The controlled release of anger is the habit of adults. Take time out to consider everything in a calm and rationale frame of mind. Be sure that you understand why the problems are occurring in the first place. If you are not sure of these, the fact is you will never be sure of what your feelings should be. Do not hesitate to speak to your partner about such questions in your mind. Communication is definitely a constructive form of the release of emotions. A simple informal chat can make one feel so much better.

It is only once you have released that your marriage can take a turn for the better. Nobody says it is easy to do so. Everybody needs to work it out in different ways since we are all made differently. Instead of harboring frustration and confusion, begin to imagine yourself feeling good. We create change from within, although we usually forget this. You will move ahead further and more quickly if you think about how good you are going to feel when you have new results. If you act from a place of confusion and upset, things do not usually turn out well.

"Before I became pregnant with our daughter, I found it difficult to live up to Dan's expectations. My family and friends told me to leave. I decided to make a list of the things I liked about Dan and the things I didn't. The scale was very unbalanced. My likes were much greater than my dislikes. I made the decision to fight for my marriage because for me the good in Dan was much more important than the bad. I let go and we now have a very happy marriage." Ossi

Our first step in making a decision is to become aware that we are making one. So many of our decisions are subconscious, and we don't even realize that we're making them. Next, notice all the areas that are affected by your ability to make decisions— your job, your health (both mind and body), your family, your relationships. The ability to make decisions affects every aspect of your life.

Begin to notice how you feel when you are making a decision. How do you feel when you have to make a decision? How well do you deal with making big decisions? After determining the many areas of life affected by your decisions and the way you feel when making them, figure out how you want to feel about making decisions (yes, even in doing this exercise you are making a decision). Do you want to feel strong and confident in your decision making? Do you want to be able to make decisions without hours of painful agonizing over what you should do?

One way to make most of your future decisions easier is to take some time right now to make some major decisions. These are going to take some consideration so take some time (a day, a week, or more if you require), and please write your answers down. We promise it will be worth the effort.

- Your destination: Where do you want to be in your relationship—what do you really want? Why do you want these things?

- Your starting point: Where are you today in your relationship?

- What do you believe in? What are your values and morals?

These powerful questions will help you to set the road map, and this book will help you to fill the gaps in your relationship. If life is a journey, these major decisions determine the destination. Without a destination, you are just wandering aimlessly through life, leaving yourself vulnerable to be blown around by the winds of fate. If you think about it, deciding on the destination determines your journey. Choose your path! It will make all the difference.

CHAPTER 1 SUMMARY

- ✓ Everything we perceive in our marriage originates in our habits and beliefs. In order to have a successful and happy marriage we have to make the decision to control the nature of our dominant, habitual thoughts and then learn how to take control on our actions and behaviors.

- ✓ The majority of couples live in a state of mass confusion. They know they're not happy and that there are issues but honestly don't know what caused their unhappiness or how to correct the problem.

- ✓ Uncovering our current beliefs is a vital part of a happy marriage. In order to uncover these beliefs, we first have to find some of their origins. From our earliest moments, any of our interactions have determined what type of spouse we'll be and consequently what kind of perceptions we will carry with us into our relationships.

- ✓ Our thoughts are the keys to a happy relationship. Thoughts control the world and as a result our marriage. To have a fulfilling marriage, it is imperative to understand the thought process.

- ✓ We try too hard to change our spouse or significant other rather than focusing on changing our own behavior. In marriage, each person needs to come to his or her own understanding of where they are NOW and what they really want.

CHAPTER 1 EXERCISE

For the next day, write down all your decisions, no matter how small. Were they conscious?

____

____

____

Did you respond or react?

____

How much more aware are you of the decisions you make after completing this exercise?

____

____

____

CHAPTER 2
THE NEW EQUATION

> *"Whether women are better than men*
> *I cannot say—but I can say they are*
> *certainly no worse".*
>
> —GOLDA MEIR

CHAPTER 2

How many times have you had a conversation about the differences between men and women? Men think women are hard to understand, and women think men are idiots. Of course we're generalizing here, but for the most part each sex has a difficult time understanding the other. When men and women get together, there are, in effect, two worlds—his and hers. They have different values, priorities, and habits. They play by different rules. Men and women differ on so many items ranging from issues as seemingly small as leaving the toilet seat up or down to much more important items such as finances.

One of the primary reasons why men and women don't seem to understand each other's differences goes back to the thought process. *Your relationship is where it is today because of your thoughts.* Are you happy and fulfilled? Do you want to spend time with your partner or drive around the block a few times after work to mentally prepare yourself for the drama that waits? No matter the case, realize that your thought can take you to a higher level in your relationship. *You will be tomorrow where your thoughts take you.*

All your relationship experiences up until now are a result of your past thoughts and beliefs, and they continue to create your future unless you decide to change them. And you can—*now*—because we're going to give you the tools to create your paradigm shift. A thought creates a feeling, which then gives rise to an emotion, and then we respond accordingly. Our goal here is to gain control of our thoughts so that we move into a consciously thought out response instead of a reaction based on our paradigms. Response, not respond. (We'll discuss this in more detail in a later chapter). When we change we create a paradigm shift by changing our thoughts we can then change our corresponding feelings, actions, and results.

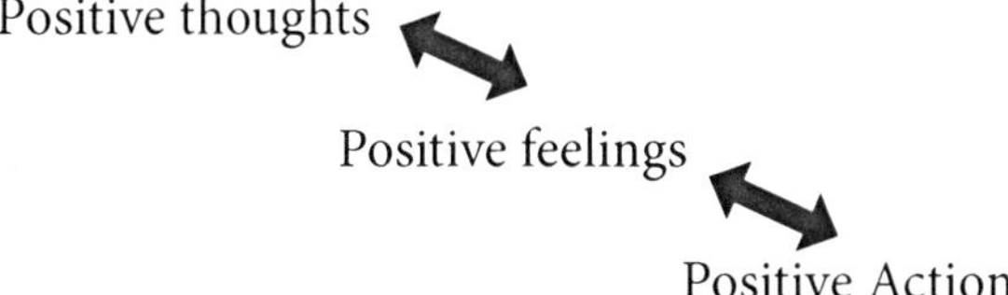

SUCCESSFUL RELATIONSHIP

Think about the above diagram for a moment. If you're not in a successful relationship, could there be an inner conflict between your thoughts, feelings, and actions? These three make the perfect equation. Your marriage can be as successful as you choose it to be, and you can be as happy as you choose to be. So doesn't it make sense to make that choice? This choice begins with a paradigm shift in which you no longer identify with past patterns of behavior and make conscious decisions to re-program your autopilot.

Few people choose their thoughts. They go through life on automatic pilot, accepting whatever comes into their mind and believing it. Creating this paradigm shift sounds easy in theory, but it is different for everyone. As a matter of fact, most people tend to think of thoughts and beliefs as one in the same. In reality, they are very different. A thought is an idea or piece of reasoning produced from thinking, while a belief, on the other hand, is set in place and more often than not based on assumptions that you've accepted as truth. Over time our thoughts form our beliefs. Your ability to transform your thoughts into new and encouraging ones depends on your past history and deep-rooted beliefs along with your determination and commitment to improving.

THE MISSING LINK

A couple was told to each write a sentence using the words sex and love. The woman wrote: "When two people love each other very much, like Samuel and I, it is morally acceptable for them to engage in sex." And Samuel wrote: "I love sex." This is typical; men and women just don't have the same thought process. So much has been said and written about relationships between men and women that it would seem impossible to add anything new to the subject. But the paradox is—no matter how much you read or consult specialists in this area, you can never find the answer to the main question: Why do men and women always compete with each other? Why can't creatures, so obviously meant to be "two halves of one whole," come to mutual understanding and happiness?

Many scientists argue that the fundamental differences between men and women are biological. It turns out that men's and women's brains, for example, are not only different, but the way we use them differs too. Women have larger connections and more frequent interaction between their brains' left and right hemispheres. This accounts for women's ability to have better verbal skills and intuition. Men, on the other hand, have greater brain hemisphere separation, which explains their skills for abstract reasoning and visual-spatial intelligence. Poet

Robert Bly describes women's brains as a "superhighway" of connection, while men's brains connections are compared to a "little crookedy country road."

Our minds think in terms of pictures. For example, if we were to ask you to think about a finger, your mind immediately envisions a mental picture of a finger. If we ask about your arm, you form a mental image of an arm. Now, if we ask you to visualize a happy relationship, what do you see? Is it your spouse and you? Or it is, perhaps, a photo of a celebrity couple in a magazine? The point of these questions is that no matter what we ask you to think of, an image instantaneously forms in your mind.

Now, let us ask you one final question. What does your mind look like? For most people, they see some sort of image resembling a medical photograph or one in an encyclopedia. This image is incorrect; what they are *actually* discerning is a picture of their brain. The mind is very different from the brain. Your brain is an organ that controls items such as body temperature and blood pressure, as well as movement. Your mind, on the other hand, is an activity found in every cell of your body. This difference distinguishes us from all other species. Our minds enable us to learn from our experiences, plan ahead, solve problems, and make decisions. We can also share information and ideas. These abilities have made us one of the most adaptable species on the planet and have enabled us to dominate it.

In order for us to have complete control over our lives, we must have an accurate picture of our mind. Dr. Thurman Fleet readily understood this concept. He was a chiropractor who believed that in order to heal his patients holistically, the entire body and mind, he must give them a clear image of the mind. After years of dedicating himself to the study of healing arts, he determined that society was approaching treatment in the wrong way. He believed that we were treating the symptoms, not the actual causes of the pain. This still holds true today. For example, if you are suffering from aches and pain in your feet or back, it is more than likely you take some sort of pain reliever rather than taking the time to analyze other causes such as fallen arches, poor posture, or even your mindset. Sadly, our medical system today isn't designed to give doctors the time to study patients' belief systems as well as their physical medical histories.

Dr. Fleet decided that since we think in terms of pictures, we need a picture of our mind. He drew a very simple picture known as the Stick Man. Even though this drawing appears simplistic in nature, it is, however, one of the most important illustrations to understand. The Stick Man is a helpful tool to explain how thoughts affect your opinion of yourself, and more importantly, this tool also enables you to see how your thoughts manifest into your reality. Understanding this "Stick Man" sketch has helped us counsel our clients with a greater amount of success. This picture brings order and understanding to your mind. So now, let us introduce you to the picture.

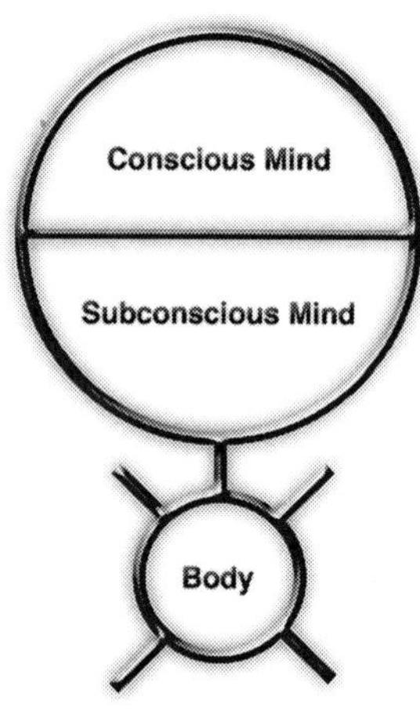

For most people, all conscious attention is on their physical body and physical results, when in fact everything we experience in our body is an expression of our mind. Since your mind is an activity, not your physical brain, it is all the more important to have a clear picture of what your mind looks like. In Dr. Fleet's drawing the head is noticeably larger than the body, suggesting that our mind has dominance over our body and not the reverse, as many would believe. Since your mind is an activity, not your physical brain, it is necessary to understand that it has two distinct parts—the conscious mind and the subconscious mind.

CONSCIOUS MIND

Our conscious mind is our thinking mind. It can accept, reject, or neglect any information and idea that comes into our it. By using our higher faculties we can create and memorize an image. Information is fed into our conscious mind through what we see, smell, hear, touch, and taste, in other words through our five senses. We also have been influenced by our environment through our five senses.

SUBCONSCIOUS MIND

A second part of our mind is our subconscious mind, which is our emotional mind. Our subconscious mind regulates all bodily sensations, such as breathing. These are hardwired into our brain, and we don't even realize that we are doing them. Here in our subconscious mind is also where our habits and belief systems are formed. The subconscious mind has no ability to reject an idea; it simply accepts every suggestion made to it as fact, and as a result our misinterpreted belief systems become ingrained into our subconscious mind. When we are very young, we either don't have our conscious mind, as in utero and up to ages 1 to 3, or it isn't developed, even up to the age of 6. We are, however, very much influenced by those closest to us as well as by our surrounding environment. At this young age, we interpret people's comments and actions very incorrectly. These interpretations have become our life belief systems.

This section of our mind is our power center. Every thought you choose to let into your subconscious mind has to become part of your subconscious mind. It has no ability to reject it. This part of us operates in an orderly manner, expressing itself through you in feelings and actions. Any thought you consciously choose to impress upon the subconscious mind over and over again becomes anchored in this part of your personality. Fixed ideas will then continue to express themselves without conscious assistance until they are replaced. These are your habits. Habits are what make you live on autopilot. When you got dressed this morning, did you need to think about how you put your clothes on? Did you need to think about how to drive your car to work? Those are all habits that reside in and are controlled by your subconscious mind. So getting dressed or brushing your teeth is so automatic that it is no longer relevant, whereas riding a horse for the first time requires thought and concentration.

Your subconscious beliefs were created by your upbringing, the environment, or any significant emotional event you may have experienced, such as an accident or a divorce. They were usually established so long ago that you're most likely unaware of them, and they include your values, beliefs, attitudes, memories, and decisions, to name a few.

Your nervous system deletes, distorts, or generalizes information based on messages from the subconscious mind. The mind only sorts what it recognizes, and that familiarity comes from experience. Even though your eyes pick up certain information, you won't see it if you're not sorting for it. Now think about this for a minute. One of our clients asked us whether or not she should leave her boyfriend or try to take their relationship to the next level. When we asked her why, she explained that she feels like his parents are involved in everything he does and are very controlling. After talking to her a bit more, we learned that she grew up in a dysfunctional family, and her perception of support and help translated into suffocation. Her boyfriend grew up in a loving and supportive environment that she did not understand. If your mind is only looking for familiar information and you grew up in a household of bad examples, what do you think you're going to see? A good example of this is a person who always dates the wrong type. He goes from one bad relationship to another. Move in, break up, move out, meet someone new, move in, break up, and move out again. He can't understand why he's in such a vicious cycle.

The answer is simple; his mind is sorting through information about relationships and looking for this type of person. Why? Because it is familiar to him. Maybe his mother did the same thing, and as a child he was shuffled from one boyfriend to the next. In addition to sorting and deleting information, our nervous system also distorts information as well. It's about creating, imagining, or interpreting information coming to you, and it explains why several people can witness the same event and all see it differently. They have a different perception based on their internal pictures, sounds, and/ or feelings. Remember the example we used in the previous chapter about the woman who got mad every time she came home from work and saw her husband sitting on the couch? She was distorting her image of him with that of her father. Her interpretation of her husband was distorted.

Along with deletions and distortions, our mind also uses generalizations as way to filter information by giving an overall theme or picture. They can be valuable by allowing you to remember and categorize your thoughts, or they can be disempowering by generalizing in ways that restrict your choices, such as "I can never be in a happy marriage." Be aware that generalizations make up your belief systems.

Memories are also stored in our subconscious mind. Our self-image is made up of memories that have an emotional connection to the past and cannot serve us when attempting to break old thought processes and habits. The subconscious mind is also the sum total of our past experiences. What we feel, think, or do forms the basis of our experiences. These are then stored in the form of subtle impressions in our subconscious mind. These impressions interact with one another and give birth to habits. We become prone to reacting in a particular way to a particular situation or stimulus depending upon the tendencies in our subconscious mind. The subconscious mind is always working; it never stops allowing us to act instinctively.

We know from neuroscience that thought produces chemical reactions in our brain, which affects our physical body by changing the way we feel. What we believe in our subconscious mind is what we feel and what is expressed through our actions. Several months ago, a woman came to us to help her fix her relationship with her daughters. They told her that she lacks the ability to give and she thought they were selfish. We asked her what the daughters say about her; they told her that she is a bitter, selfish, and vengeful person. We then asked her how she deals with this type of a person. Her answer to us was, "You stay away from them." This is exactly how her daughters treated her. They avoided her.

Our actions are what give us our results, and in the case of the mother, she acted in a manner that resulted in her daughters avoiding her. So if you want to know what you are thinking subconsciously, simply look at your results. And if you want to change the results you are getting, you need to change what you think about. Most people look at their results as their potential. This is not accurate. *The results we have been getting up until now are merely a reflection of our past thoughts* is the old model. Once we learn to create healthy and abundant images in our mind of what we now desire, our results will reflect those images of the new model.

Since your subconscious mind has no choice but to accept your thoughts as reality, it has to then accept the stream of pictures you provide it as truth. A great analogy for this portion of the mind is one of a garden. Think of a beautiful garden filled with all sorts of vibrantly colored flowers. To maintain your garden's grandeur, you must spend a great deal of time pulling weeds. If you don't, soon the weeds will overtake the flowers. Our subconscious mind is much like this garden. These weeds are our erroneous belief systems of how we see ourselves and others. They suffocate any productive thoughts such as "I am capable and competent" and replace them with "I'm not good enough."

We have quite a number of negative images, many of which pertain to our relationships. These seeds were planted in our garden, the subconscious mind, when we didn't know how not to let them in. By replanting healthy thoughts, you now can change your actions and live a healthier life. The more aware we become of these limiting thoughts, the easier it is to change them. If we don't consciously choose our thoughts, we'll be replaying our parents' marriage or someone else's we had as an example. A plane can only fly on autopilot for so long;

eventually the pilot is going to have to come back and take control, or the plane will crash. A relationship is no different. Your subconscious mind will steer you in the direction it wants you to go based on your past experiences, beliefs, and habits. It will give you more of the same. If you're choosing to make changes in your life—to do things differently and achieve different results—then it's your job to make sure that your conscious mind is guiding your actions. Make the decision to change your thinking and you will then change your paradigm and your results. You are one step away from taking control and steering your life—vision your *ideal relationship* and act.

BODY

The smallest portion of Dr. Fleet's drawing is the body. It is the instrument of the mind, the house you live in, the thoughts and images that are consciously chosen. For example, fear of a disease, worry, happy with our lives, etc. Impressing a thought upon the subconscious mind (which is every cell of your body) moves your body into action. These actions you are involved in determine your results.

But there is one problem with The Stick Man—it is a man. We need to give him a Stick Woman just as God gave Adam an Eve.

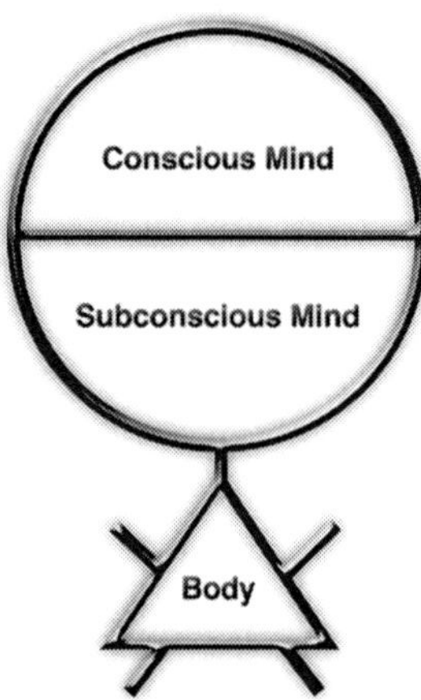

Now that we know what our mind looks like, we also understand that a man's and a woman's mind are one and the same; we share the same mind, but our thoughts and feelings are different, driving different actions. Actually, this is true for any person. Women act a certain way and men act a certain way. Throughout all of history we've subconsciously been programmed to believe that a man is one way and a woman is another way. This belief has been influenced by our parents, the environment, religion, kings and leaders, and any other authority figures. These beliefs are a product of a long, deep history.

What if we could combine the Stick Man and Stick Woman to create a third mind where we acknowledge that both of us have different thoughts but have the same beliefs about them? During our seminars we tell the participants that 1+1=3, and they look at us like we're crazy. This new equation is a result of us combining our minds and creating a third mind. You see, we each need to be an individual with our own thoughts, but as a couple we need to become one, sharing the same feelings and beliefs. The new equation of our mind is the same that opens the possibility for a harmonic marriage.

MAKE THE SHIFT

One of our favorite quotes is Earl Nightingale's "You become what you think about." With choice you are no longer the victim of your subconscious thinking and filters. Remember, you can't change the way your partner thinks, but you can change the way you think. Who you are right now doesn't have to reflect who you choose to be in the future. Are the thoughts, beliefs, and habits that supported you earlier still appropriate in your relationship? Or have you outgrown them?

You can have the relationship you desire if you change your thinking. Just release the beliefs that are holding you back. The only limitation is in your mind. Everything you face externally is a manifestation of what's going on within. Look beyond your circumstances. You are responsible for how you respond or react in your marriage. Identify what you're thinking about, and as you monitor your thoughts, see how they affect the way you feel and act.

If your thoughts no longer support you, rather than trying to eliminate negative thinking, which would put your focus on what you don't want, concentrate on what we call truth-based thinking. This is nothing more than choosing to accept only those thoughts that support you in what you're trying to achieve, once you know who you are and how you want your relationship to be. It's not just about being positive or negative—positive and negative thinking are both determined largely by your belief system, and many of your beliefs were influenced by others long ago. Truth-based thinking comes from being aware, having your antennae up, and understanding the reality of any given situation. It's about discernment and personal truth, and when you're true to yourself, you'll have an open and honest relationship.

What happens when you try truth-based thinking and you fall back into the trap of sabotaging thoughts? Realize it was the action or behavior that didn't work; your attempt failed, not you, and the great news is that you have another chance to do it better next time! When this happens, attach a new meaning to event and turn the negative into positive. For instance, tell yourself that you may have fallen back into an old erroneous belief, but you were able to create an awareness of the destructive pattern of thought.

All of us make "mistakes"—they happen to be an essential part of the learning process. It's when you don't take heed and continue to make the same mistake that it's time to question what's going on! There is no failure in life, only feedback. Trust your mistakes and see them as a gift from the Universe designed to steer you in the right direction. Bring them on as you grow and evolve into the best relationship possible. The process of becoming aware of your negative thoughts may seem difficult at first, but it does become more habitual as you practice. Repetition reinforces, so don't give up. Stay focused on your new pattern of thinking—you're rewiring your brain by withering the old neural paths and building a new neural network. As you send different messages to your subconscious mind it starts to filter for success, and you see successes more and more in your life. Take gradual steps, like the joke goes: How do you eat an elephant? One bite at a time. Creating a paradigm shift is a gradual process, but with each belief you replace you're one step closer to success.

Your reality is not reality, it's merely your perception of reality—how you see a situation based on your beliefs, past experiences, values, habits, attitude, identity, all that has shaped your internal filter. **Your reality can be changed.** We all have the power of choice. You choose how you respond or react to any situation, either consciously or subconsciously. You can dwell on the past or you can release. You can become conscious and aware and you can have the relationship you've always dreamed of, not the one you grew up with. Our subconscious minds would rather experience pain than traverse unknown territory, and until you decide to change and develop a *new level of awareness*, you're going to have the same results not only in your relationship but in the rest of your life as well.

CHAPTER 2 SUMMARY

✓ Men and women have different values, priorities, and habits. They differ on so many items ranging from issues seemingly as small as leaving the toilet seat up or down to much more important items such as finances.

✓ People in unsuccessful relationships have inner conflict between their thoughts, feelings, and actions. Our marriage can be as successful as we choose it to be, and we can be as happy as we choose to be once we no longer identify with past patterns of behavior and make conscious decisions to reprogram our thoughts.

✓ The mind is very different from the brain and has two distinct parts—the conscious mind and the subconscious mind.

✓ Our conscious mind has the ability to accept, reject, or neglect any information or idea that comes into our mind. Information is fed into our conscious mind through our five senses.

✓ Our subconscious mind accepts every suggestion made to it as fact. Our subconscious mind is also where our habits and belief systems are formed.

✓ As individuals we need to have our own thoughts but as a couple we need to become one, sharing the same feelings and beliefs, which results in a harmonic marriage.

CHAPTER 2 EXERCISE

For the next day pay close attention to your thoughts throughout the day and write them in a journal—all of them!

____

____

____

____

Mark only positive thoughts that will improve your relationship.

For the next 48 hours read and focus on the positive thoughts that you have selected. Is there an improvement in your thinking? Notice a pattern emerging, either negative or positive, indicating where to direct your attention. It can actually be quite surprising. When you acknowledge your habitual way of thinking you can change your thought process and replace negative and false beliefs.

CHAPTER 3
OPEN YOUR MIND TO ALL THAT IS

"Love is blind — marriage
is the eye-opener".

–Pauline Thomason

CHAPTER 3

Do we plan and control our own relationship, or do we find ourselves led into it? As a young couple, we never actually talked about our duality; instead we focused mainly on the future and what we didn't have. We didn't have any joint goals; one of us wanted to go one way and the other wanted to go in a different direction. We tried marriage counseling, but what we found was that it focused on what we were doing wrong and didn't give us a solution. We didn't want to hear about our failures. Once we finally understood that to create a relationship was based on the beliefs we inherited from our parents and environment, we realized only then that we could stop repeating our mistakes and move forward in our relationship, but we still missed one critical piece of the relationship puzzle.

Now that we know what our mind looks like, and that we are not just a stick man and a stick woman but instead a third mind while at the same time maintaining our individual thoughts and feelings. Here's a simple and basic example: When a man thinks of relations the feeling usually chosen is sex, and when a woman thinks of relations, the feeling is romance.

So, their actions will be different; he wants to move into "action" while she wants to kiss, dance, have a glass of wine, and then move into "action." So how do we close the gap between the two feelings? We do so through mental foreplay. Action is what we call mental foreplay. To do so, however, we have to reach a certain level of awareness because with awareness comes the solution.

Awareness isn't just about relationships. It applies to every issue of our life. We may have a high level of awareness in our professional life but a very low level in our personal life. We have to make a conscious effort to increase our awareness in every level of our life. For the purpose of this book, however, we're going to focus on raising your level of awareness in your marriage. Many of our clients ask us to describe awareness. We compare awareness to a radio transmitter and receiver. When your radio transmitter is adjusted correctly you'll be able to receive any station you desire, while on the other hand, if it is too far away or not working correctly, you'll just hear static. With the highest level of awareness we can gain a true perspective on each other and live a fulfilled life together.

Another way to view on a scale from 1 to 10 where are your thoughts right now—10 is 100% in the present and 1 is 100% wondering (dream walker).

After 30 years of marriage, we have reached a level of harmony, and at times it is a bit scary to realize that we have achieved the third mind. For us, we believe that everything is doable, there are no goals that can't be accomplished, and we live in an environment of unselfish love and giving. While mastering our thoughts and results to infinite awareness, this is all new for us. We still have much to explore in this potential. Mastering your level of awareness can take you beyond your wildest dreams.

WHERE DO YOU DIRECT YOUR ATTENTION

Awareness—why is it so important? Ignorance allows life to appear in a way that takes control over our thoughts. There is a story about a bird that falls to the ground and lands in a pile of cow shit. The bird is warm but still a bit uncomfortable and looking for a way out. A wolf comes along and cleans up the bird. He thinks to himself, "Finally, I feel so much better" while only a few seconds later the wolf eats him. The moral of this story is that someone who shits on you may be your friend while the one who cleans you up can very well be your enemy. We tend to live in a comfort zone even if it is a "shitty" one. We make the same mistakes only to find out that the ones who are trying to help us don't always have our best interests at heart. In our case, it was a marriage counselor and family and friends. While we continually shat on each other those closest to us tried to sabotage our relationship.

Have you ever realized that you keep repeating the same "mistakes" over and over" despite your best efforts to make changes with or without the intervention of anyone else? Most often you have no idea why you self-sabotage and bring about those unwanted results. You've probably thought to yourself, "Here we go again, the same argument." In this case "you" continue to view the situation in a way that gives rise to old patterns of self-sabotaging the relationship. This behavior may stem from a belief that you're not good enough, so subconsciously you set about to prove that, all the time totally unaware of the driving force. With this lack of awareness, how can the result be any different? It's best to get it right the first time, otherwise it keeps coming back to bite you in the ass. Until you learn the lesson, you're going to be living the same life over and over again.

Just because you repeat the same mistakes doesn't mean that you're not smart or that you're ignorant. Awareness is about being conscious, not ignorant. It's about having knowledge. You can't change what you don't acknowledge. Our intention in writing this book is to help you and your partner feel informed, inspired, and empowered by giving you all the tools and techniques to free yourself from your paradigms that have stifled your growth, to love and accept yourself and your partner, and to have the relationship of your dreams. To accomplish this, however, you must first become aware of where to direct your attention. When you acknowledge that your pattern of behavior isn't working, you have a choice: keep doing what you're doing or change! So the first step for transformation and growth is to change your level of awareness.

How can you improve your relationship if you don't recognize opportunities to do so? The definition of insanity is doing the same thing over and over again and expecting different results. Or if you ignore the fact that perhaps your opinion is a little out of date or that maybe there's a better way of doing things. We're not in any way implying that your relationship be "fixed" because you're broken! None of us are broken; we are instead only a reflection of our past beliefs. All beliefs and paradigms can be changed once you make the conscious decision to do so. Are there some areas in your life—maybe the way you treat others or even the way you think about certain things like your self-image, your relationship with your spouse, or your views on raising a family, for example—that you could choose to see, do, or think about differently and more constructively, with a level of awareness and openness to another point of view?

Conversely, when you're aware that you have an underlying habit that's not serving you, you're in an empowered state to change your thinking, which of course leads to improved results. Again, the choice is yours: keep doing what you're doing or change! You see, awareness is fundamental, along with the willingness to accept that change is necessary for improved results and the flexibility to expand beyond your current self-imposed limitations and beliefs. Our goal in this chapter is to teach you how to expand your awareness, but first let us introduce you to the seven levels of awareness.

THE SEVEN LEVELS OF AWARENESS

Animal React vs. Respond. At this level all we do is respond to our spouse's actions / behavior and are controlled only by our five senses. Instead of responding to certain situations with controlled thoughts, we just react and blurt out the first words that come to mind. The same is true with actions. Sure, when someone makes you angry, you may want to hit him, but if you're operating at a higher level of awareness you'll instead remain calm and try to rationalize with him. Operating at the animal level decreases your ability to process information; you always act from an emotional state and let the circumstances control you.

Ask yourself whether you react to what is happening or whether you absorb, analyze, and form a response mentality, Do you find yourself reacting to what you see? For example: There is a mess in the house. You go in to find your spouse stretched supine on the couch. You instantly respond to the smell of the dirty laundry piled up. Or you come home from work and want Chinese food for dinner, and you react badly when you see you're having a schnitzel with fried potatoes.

As we see things only through our senses, we have limited ability to grow and develop. If you think about it, it is a selfish level. We try to force our spouse to think like us; we try and often succeed in convincing ourselves that we truly are right. Sometimes we exceed ourselves trying to think about what our spouse would think and do in a certain situation, but habits (paradigm) take control of our feelings at this point, and we find ourselves dismissing the idea to begin with. We are convinced of our rightness, which leads us into ongoing conflicts within the relationship system. Each of us is locked in our own position and viewpoint.

The only difference between us and other animals is the ability to reason, so when we are controlled by our five senses we are not different from any other animal. Moving beyond the animal level is important because we view our surroundings and our entire world from a narrow and limited perception. We controlled by our emotions (paradigms); at this stage there is a short between the senses and feelings and the environment stimulating flows directly into our feelings, causing us to react. People living at this level usually don't have any goals or desire to succeed.

Mass – Conform. At this level we live our life by copying others—we do what other people do. We follow the crowd and have no independent thoughts of our own. We're like a herd of sheep being led to slaughter. We took a vacation with another couple several years back, and all they did was argue. The man asked us why we didn't yell at one another like everyone else does, and we said that we do argue but not in front of everyone. We prefer to keep our arguments private. Outside pressure affects couples and begins to loosen up the fight. Couples look at other couples and say, "Why can't we be like them?"

At this point of awareness, we start to think that we need to be like everyone else we know, and we have much to learn from others. But this is not the case—we need to find out who we want to be, and learn from those who made it. Once you base your actions and thoughts on others like you, you've reached the second or next to lowest level—the mass stage. You're swept away by your surrounding environment. You want to buy a bigger house, a newer car like your neighbors, and soon you yourself in an endless cycle of purchase and acquisitions. All of our behavior is an impression of others, and we imitate others' thinking that they know better. Our children quickly absorb it, creating their own pressure; we find ourselves doing things without any self-thinking or consideration. If you've recognized yourself in either of these two stages we've just talked about, you're not ready for a relationship. Worse still, if one of these stages represents you, you're in a relation-shit, and you definitely should keep reading about how to move up to the next level.

Aspiration – Desire. Initially, we find ourselves living the lives of our parents, and as we mature we move on and want to live the lives of those surrounding us. We can't go through life imitating others, and eventually we find that we want more out of life. We start to realize that life has more to offer and that we deserve it. But there is one problem—we know what we want, we just don't know how to get it.

Why this is happening? Simple, because when we see in our mind the image of the new relationship we want, this is great, but we use the old tools we have to create something new, something which is, in our mind, currently impossible. Therefore, we have a picture of what we want; at this point our emotions come into action tell us that we are not going to get it, that we cannot do it, and so on. We rarely see things as they are in reality. We are emotionally victims of situations that have happened to us in the past.

An experience with a marriage counselor is a great example of this level of awareness. Most couples at the desire stage seek counseling. The first question they're asked by the marriage counselor is: What do you want? But the problem is you really don't know what you want; up until this point all of your needs and desires have been based on your paradigms. You can change for a week, two weeks, but soon or later those old paradigms are going to creep back in and take over your life again.

When we come to stage where we understand that something is missing, we want to change our reality, we want more. This step brings us to the desire for knowledge. Once you realize you want something different in life, take the time to study, learn, and seek out who you really want to be, not who others think you should be. At this stage, all of your actions are moving you toward your true goals and authentic self.

Enroll in relationship workshops, read books, and study. The reason this situation happens is the will of desire develops into something else. Actually, this reminds us of the reason why we began a new stage in our relationship. We both had a desire to change. We were unwilling to settle with the current situation and needed to find an alternative to move forward. We created a new image in our minds, where we saw the new relationship system. This is a critical stage where we seek help from the outside. Most of us find it in a form of an external experts, literature, and workshops. Ask yourself: Is this the only way our relationship can be?

Individual – Uniqueness. At this level of awareness independent thinking is the step that will help us to create positive changes in our lives. The way to do this is to find the cause that holds us from taking actions or making a move to the next step in our journey to get to the next level. We feel that a marriage is like a tree, and we grow as individuals just as the branches grow separate from the trunk. The trunk though is the heart of the tree that keeps it alive by supplying nutrients and water to the branches. It is okay to be independent, but remember, you must have a common vision for the marriage.

Relationship consultants and workshops may address the point of need to change individual behaviors. Usually this is true and it might help, but it is always temporary. Behaviors are not the reason. The real reason, rather, is the paradigms that control our lives, our feelings, our approach, and most important, our results. If you have not already noticed that something is missing, now is a good time to ask, "So what about love, what role does it play? What about sex, where does it come into this picture? And romance, how to use it?"

Well, now is the time to put it in a correct perspective and content. Sex, love, and romance are feelings. Paradigms are feelings. The same is true for fear, hate, jealousy, disappointment, happiness, and any other feelings. Our paradigms control all the results in our lives and are the emotions raised from our subconsciousness by the thoughts we choose.

A thought, based on our experience, will choose a certain (always the same) emotion we know. For each thought there is a specific feeling. A thought about our spouse in a certain way will bring an emotion of sex, the same thought about a friend or a movie star might also do the trick. Sex is one of the most powerful emotions (similar to the belief). This emotion must be controlled and channeled; in a relationship sex can be great but also destructive if not controlled. Sex mixed with love will create a wonderful feeling in a more controlled and less aggressive environment. It brings up the feeling of partnership. A final touch will be added by romance will also prevent another disaster, and bring harmony into our lives.

Feelings are paradigms that can wake unbridled sex or gentle love, blinded jealousy or happiness; all of them are controlled by our subconscious and roused by conscious thoughts. At this stage it is time to align and organize your thoughts and feelings in pairs. Good thoughts plus good feelings planted into our subconscious allows us to create new results and grow toward our goals.

Discipline – Command and Act. Most people spend their entire lives making decisions that prevent them from moving forward. The level of discipline starts at a point we as a couple decide on as a mutual vision. Couples may come to us and say: "We thought that having a mutual vision and a common goals means having an equal way of thinking." How does it correlate? The answer is that the empowering one another comes from polarity and opposite opinions. The carry out action must be done in full cooperation.

Discipline comes into meaning when you begin doing things constantly. Changes in our relationship started when we decided on something together and did so together. For example, we decided on and executed a trip abroad. That taught us that acting on our decisions causes results; now all that was missing was the "how."

It appears that most people keep planning, not moving to action, because there is no decision and of course no action; the way seems to be long and sometimes impossible. Think about a couple that continues to plan without following through. They talk about building a new house but never do. They talk about exercising and eating healthy but never do. How do you think that affects their relationship? Lack of action can stagnate a relationship and can last for years.

Successful couples make fast decisions. We recommend using the self-questioning method:

1. Do we really want it?
2. Will it move us in the direction of our vision / goal?

If the answers are "yes," make a plan to fulfill your decision. A couple needs to find a mutual purpose and a vision and follow through on fulfilling it. When we find ourselves having an idea, making a conscious decision based on the questions above, we can move on to the next level.

Experience – Continued Learning. The more we act on our decisions the more experience we gain. So what exactly is the level of experience? It's a state where there are many ideas, and it is easy to make yes or no decisions. The rest is done by the subconscious mind. Therefore, as you gain more experience, the autopilot kicks into action, getting you to your destination. Look at it as driving; we remember the days of learning how to drive, we need to think of the many actions required. Every action started as a thought, even for a simple action such as shifting gear. Today you enter a car and get to where you want almost without a single conscious thought. It's true there are doubts that never disappear, but it doesn't matter because you continuously improve your awareness, so use your imagination to see your goal, your will to hold up the thought intuition, and let your intuition do the rest.

With experience we create an idea, see a mental picture, and make it into a reality. What truly brought us to this level is our confidence in how much the other has grown. We admire each other's abilities equally and see ourselves through each other's eyes. We keep educating ourselves. We continue to evolve. It is not a coincidence that we find ourselves saying the same sentences. Although our thoughts may be different our actions are the same.

We think and act on the same level; therefore our actions are similar. When we coach people, they see a synergy among us, which empowers them. With experience comes the level of expertise, and we're fortunate enough to be able to teach others how we've risen above and beyond this level of awareness.

Mastery – Respond vs. React. This level of infinite awareness comes from mastering our thoughts and results in creating the life we dream of and enjoying the process of living it. We respond rather than react. At this level, we've mastered the decision process and no longer live our lives on autopilot. We are constantly evolving and are no longer afraid to move beyond our comfort zone. We are no longer the stick man or a stick woman; we've formed the third mind. Everything we do as a couple is a unique creation designed to move our relationship forward. At this level, we are able to guide and mentor others.

SEVEN STEPS TO GREATER AWARENESS

*Success or failure is a decision,
happiness or depression is the way to
the decision.*

—Dan

You now understand the various levels of awareness and what to expect as you move up the scale. The following are eight steps to get you there.

1. Be willing to accept that change is necessary.

2. Be flexible to expand beyond your comfort zone. There are dozens of ways of doing things, all of them leading to the same result. Is it possible that you could be limiting yourself to one way of seeing, thinking, and feeling—the same path you've always taken? Why not be flexible, have courage, and trust and take the next step up the levels of awareness? You may not always choose "correctly" in your opinion, but you can make better choices.

3. Release your paradigms and see your relationship as it really is.

4. See so-called "failures" as opportunities, understanding that growth leads to greater challenges, which leads to a high level of awareness. Keep in mind that cultivating awareness is a never-ending process. Always live in a quest for knowledge and most importantly, apply that knowledge to increase your level of awareness in your relationship.

5.   Act consciously and stop making the same self-sabotaging decisions. Make it a point to be open to new information and new concepts and put them into practice. You'll never know if you don't strive to evolve to the highest level of awareness. There are so many more options when you expand your awareness and stay alert. If you feel a sense of discontent, ask powerful questions such as, "What am I searching for? Who do I know who can guide me?" hen listen to the answers; trust your intuition—it knows what's best for you.

6.   Remember, you can't change anything you don't acknowledge. One of our favorite quotes is: "Minds are like parachutes, they are best when they are open." Challenge your beliefs and feelings and become aware of them because they are indicators of what is happening on the "inside." Just by noticing your behavior you become aware of what might be blocking your happiness, and you can choose to change. The only constant is change, and if you're willing to expand your level of awareness, you'll get the relationship of your dreams. Change, however, does take time, and that time varies for each and every one of you according to your own particular circumstances and the effort you put in.

7.   The key is to be persistent and patient, knowing that if you keep doing the work and applying the techniques daily you'll reach the Mastery Level—when your thoughts, feelings, and actions are in harmony. Expand your awareness and open your mind to all that is.

8.   Make a decision to learn how to constantly improve your mental faculties (Chapter 5)

CHAPTER 3 SUMMARY

- ✓ **Animal react vs. respond.** At this level all we do is respond to our spouse's actions / behavior and are controlled only by our five senses. Instead of responding to or acting toward certain situations with controlled thoughts, we just react and blurt out the first words that come to mind. At this level we act from an emotional state and let circumstances control us.

- ✓ **Mass – Conform.** At this level we follow the crowd and have no independent thoughts of our own. At this point of awareness, we believe that we have much to learn from others.

- ✓ **Aspiration – Desire.** At this level we start to realize that life has more to offer and that we deserve to have more.

- ✓ **Individual – Uniqueness.** At this level of awareness independent thinking is the step that will help us to create positive changes in our lives.

- ✓ **Discipline – Command and Act.** At this level, as couples we decide and act toward a mutual vision.

- ✓ **Experience – Continued Learning.** At this level we create an idea, make a decision, and act.

- ✓ **Mastery – Respond vs. React.** At this level of infinite awareness we respond rather than react and are no longer afraid to move beyond our comfort zone. We master our thoughts actions and results to create the life we dream of and to enjoy the process of living it.

CHAPTER 3 EXERCISE

Determine what level of relationship awareness you are currently living in.

____

____

Create one commitment that will elevate you to the next level.

____

____

Write it down and share with your spouse .

____

____

CHAPTER 4
FOREPLAY FOR THE MIND

*"Men marry women with the hope
they will never change. Women marry
men with the hope they will change.
Invariably they are both disappointed".*

—ALBERT EINSTEIN

CHAPTER 4

Something deep inside keeps us from changing. Something prevents us from believing in ourselves enough to have the relationship of our dreams. What is it? What keeps us from being happy? Successful? It simple really—if you don't believe you can do something then your behavior will reflect that belief.

"Insecurity is a major component of many relationships; I had a lot of it. It stemmed from the fact that I did not get much positive feedback from those closest to me. I only knew when I was doing something wrong; then the reaction was strong, it felt like a slap in the face, but when I did something good, it just went through, no response at all. Life taught me to want little more, but I had bigger dreams. The change point started when I decided to change and pursue my dream and never give up. One of the positive paradigms that helped me, as my mother told me, is that when I was born, the taxi driver who took us home from the hospital told my mother that I will have lots of luck. This story made me believe that I do."Ossi

Every moment of our lives is affected in one way or another by our thoughts. Before we can move forward we have to have foreplay for the mind, which is what we have found to be a winning strategy for harmony in relationships. Why do we believe this to be such a good strategy? Simple. When you have foreplay for the mind you have three essential items for a successful relationship. They are:

- Clarity

- Understanding

- Action

When we think and talk about our desire to earn money, for instance, we are not really thinking about or discussing money at all. You see, we actually are looking for freedom and liberty from money neediness. We want the ability to do as we want. The same is true for our health. We can say or think whatever we want, but the underlying thought is the same as money. We actually want to be free from illness or any health issues. When we're healthy, we're free to do come as go and don't have to depend on anyone for help.

Relationships are different, however. We want a satisfying relationship to be part of our life and to provide harmony and fulfill our being. Once we achieve this type of a connection it will move us from fear of loneliness to sharing and loving. Most couples think that this is the winning point of the relationship because at this stage they think they've found the key to a successful and happy marriage.

But in reality, it is also the point where couples come to the understanding that they have no back-up plan and no alternative. What used to work till now doesn't work anymore, but couples are afraid to break the status quo, as they might sabotage the relationship. This stage reminds us of the possum. To protect itself from enemies and survive, the possum pretends to be dead until danger is over. Most of the time it works, but there are always exceptions.

The same thing happens in marriage. You might find a system that works for you. For instance, many of the women we counsel learn that submission is a kind of control. By this we mean that submissive behavior is a way to avoid arguments. If a wife constantly agrees with her husband to his face and then goes and does whatever she wants behind his back she feels as though she's in control. Regardless of the fact that the people around her think the opposite and that she is totally wrong, for her the system works; this is what important. The same goes for the spouse; he perceives that having the last word works for him—it's his winning point, and he will do everything to get there.

"Several years ago, I received a promotion that frightened me very much. It involved a major life change in which I would have had to move to an office in another country. I knew I wanted it but was afraid of it at the same time. So the only thing I knew to do was to jump into the role and hope for the best. I also knew I could not do it without the support of Ossi. She supported me and we took on the new challenge. Sometimes it felt like we were drowning, waiting for someone to throw us a rope, and sometimes we felt so good, like we deserved to win a medal. Unfortunately, in relationship there are no medals or goblets, at least not tangible ones. In life, same as in relationship, we learn to swim only after we jump into the water. But when you succeed in your marriage and it feels so good it's like you won the best trophy of all." Dan

THREE DOORS, THREE BRAINS

Our life is all about the physical, emotional, and mental states we live in. These three states correlate to our three brains. Yes, it is true we have three brains, not just one. They include:

1. The **REPTILIAN** brain. We are born with it. It is not influenced by culture or personal history. It deals with

survival and reproduction. It is the center for instinctive reflexes, primitive impulses, sex, and violence. We know from history that the Reptilian brain always wins.

2. The **LIMBIC** brain, acquired during the beginning of human life (ages 0-5) is in relationship with the mother. It is the center of emotion, representing tensions, feelings, and contradictions.

3. The **CORTEX**, usually in place around age 7, is the center of rational thinking. It is the logic tool that we use to look at the world: science, logic, control, numbers, statistics, money, and <u>intellectual ability.</u>

Now that we know that we have three brains, how are we going to take advantage of that in our relationship? We can awaken it in a positive way through our five senses. There isn't a conscious procedure. Everything is subconscious. If we don't know why, usually it comes from the reptilian brain. If someone does something and it's not clear, not understandable, and seems extreme, it's a sign we awakened that part of the brain. If we understand this place, we can be in control, and we can aim the conversation. It's like an animal that is angry, and we're trying to calm it down. We must keep it happy. We're doing it through food, shelter, and a pat on the head.

The second door is the limbic brain. This door is a feeling, and what's stopping us is our fear, for example, a fear of losing love. This fear makes us be alert instead of being open to our spouse. When they need support and love, we criticize them. When we envision a relationship, it translates to hard work. We invest our time and effort and at times wonder what happens if it doesn't work for us. Once this happens, we begin to make all kinds of assumptions, especially negative ones. Assumptions in a relationship are like termites. You don't see anything, but suddenly the house is torn apart. The influence of our parents and authority in our life also has an influence on this door. Did we receive love? Do we have the need to show love or not? There is a fear of consequences. We deal with the fear of result as if we are doing everything possible, but we are disappointed in the results. Here is where the love language is going into action. We choose who we are in a conversation, like being confident, funny, loving; we decide how the conversation will end, and we allow the other person to get emotionally taxed from the conversation.

The third door, the cortex, is where consciousness gets in. We use imagination and logic in order to create meaningful moments in our marriage in the present. We create in the present so we'll have optimistic memories about the past so that we can build our future. It's our ability to catch from distance a situation and be like a fly on the wall, see from a far distance the truth and then decide. It helps us decide what kind of things we allow to enter into our life, and it's our ability of perception. If we're using info that's given to us from our partner along with info from ourselves, we're getting a larger picture and arguments are prevented. We're both right.

Each of us has our own perception. Together we complete the picture. Actually, we pass through our three doors every day. When we wake up in the morning, our procedure, we need to pass the three doors in order to control our result. At this stage, we know our partner. We can sit and write down all circumstances that awaken him to extreme reaction. In order to pass through the first door, we need to make sure that our appearance is a nice appearance externally. Smile, willingly avoid unwanted reaction of the reptile brain. Good atmosphere, sex, will usually come with the animal reaction. The second door, the limbic door, is the door of being present and getting new habits and the language of love. This is the most important part of the relationship; we adapt new habits that will become an automatic daily ritual that will assure our success in creating the relationship that we want. The third door, the cortex, is intellectual stimulation, conversation, created pictures; it stimulates the imagination and a lot of new things in the relationship that will stimulate and open the third door.

To improve our physical, emotional, and mental lifestyle we need to learn to love ourselves (clarity), become aware of the law of attraction—like attracts alike (understanding)—and create positive and optimistic moments in our present relationship (action).

By correlating our three brains with our three doors we can create an environment of definite success in our relationship through the creation of shared goals and a supportive environment and set up the atmosphere to make sure that we can't «fail to improve» our relationship. Remember, to be loved is to take responsibility and control over this ability. *Below are just a few stories of the many couples we've helped bring harmony to their relationships.*

A woman's first husband was chosen by her mother. When she came to us her belief was that love is not long-lasting. Although she wanted a relationship, she had no idea how to create one. When she spoke of relationships her descriptions of her mate reflected her beliefs. She believed she wanted someone who was the opposite of her first husband. She wanted a rich businessman because she thought he would be interested by his knowledge and not bored. She therefore attracted emotionally shallow men who were rich businessmen and kept repeating the same pattern. All she was looking for were men who fit her reptilian brain—good looking—and met her cortex brain—intellectual—and she skipped her second or limbic brain, the emotional system. In our conversations with her we revitalized her emotional system through her parents. For her, her parents' relationship was based on something she wanted to run away from. She experienced continuous and endless arguments between her parents and as a child played the role of the mediator. Therefore, all she knew of relationships was from the perspective of her childhood experience, and because her mother obligated her to choose her side, it turns out that she not only was fighting for her own personal relationship, but she was fighting not to be like her mother and to not attract a man like her father. When we helped her to see a different side of her parents' relationship, and that her parents were really connected by immense love without knowledge of how to maintain it, all she experienced was the expressed frustration. Now she could start to forgive.

Of course as a result, her relationship with her parents significantly improved and her ability to find a partner who would change her pattern of belief that love ends was now easy for her. The man she found answered all her desires. She began to use the three-brain system in order to find her new husband. The man she eventually found was actually in her life for a long time, yet never saw him as a potential mate. Only when she became familiar with her real needs and wants was she able to begin a relationship with him. So, what gives hope to people is that the partner you are looking for may not be far away or unknown but may be near. But you may be stuck and unable to utilize the three brains in order to find your true love.

Another woman of a married couple, who we had already helped to build a successful business, called us urgently requesting help with her marriage since her husband had recently left her. We held individual conversations with each and found that the wife felt that since her husband had become an entrepreneur he therefore should have more time to spend at home with her and their children than he did when he was a salaried employee. He, however, expressed that she needed to improve her time management in her independent work and also felt that she should be more involved with the home and kids. Through utilizing the tools of the Language of Love we helped them to ultimately realize that they each really desired more time with each other even though neither had said so. They wanted more time, more attention, and to feel less judgment in their relationship. Once we were able to help them communicate they discovered that they each wanted to be heard without response, and this opened the door both in their relationship and for him to return to their home. How many of us are really in a process of listening rather than a process of response? Often times in our communications, the other may not be speaking in order to receive a response of advice but just to be listened to. One reason why so many people in the world communicate with God is because He is the best listener.

A couple who attended one of our relationship seminars declared themselves as a level 6 in their awareness. They found themselves dealing with unexpected difficulties communicating with their 17 year-old daughter. All of their conversations with her were through yelling, resistance, misunderstanding, etc. They decided they were going to give up on her the moment she left for college. Through the Language of Love and our teachings, we helped them to speak through their true feelings and not the anger that masked it. They were able to understand that their daughter wanted what every child does, which is love and to be heard. She in return was able to give them a calm house void of uncontrolled anger. Once the parents understood the effect of the Language of Love on their home, they perceived their marriage differently than they had in the start. They realized that their own relationship was based on competition and control and that there were many things they wanted to communicate but feared to do so. Their inability to communicate was the reason why they had initially viewed themselves as a level 6 when in reality they were a level 3, that of aspirations, and had work to accomplish in their relationship. They put into action the lessons of the seminars and private meetings and greatly improved their marriage. As a result they not only bettered their relationship but were able to manifest longstanding goals in business they had previously been unable to attain as a result of the blockages in their relationship.

Another woman came to us after bad divorce and a bad relationship that was violent—mentally violent. After she got courage and got a divorce, the last thing she thought about was a new relationship, but life has its own rhythm. Time passed and one day she decided she deserved a new relationship. Going backward in her belief system, she thought she was a princess. What she tried to find before was someone rich and good looking, but she had no idea what the meaning of intimacy, listening, and honor was. From her point of view, what was between her father and mother was unconditional love, and she thought that's what she was getting. What we taught her was that she needed to focus on what she really wants and connected it to the five ingredients. She described the man that she wanted through the three brains, from the outside, from feeling, and from his mental ability. In a short period of time she found this guy that was actually around her for the last twenty years. She hadn't been able, with the knowledge that she had and her belief system and her vulnerability from her last relationship, to see him or find him, but we worked with her to change her belief system and her self-esteem; it was true love, and they are together to this day. The message is to not what you're missing in a relationship but what you want. As you know less what you want, don't be surprised if that's what you're getting.

We are talking about one of the essences, which is one of the ingredients, which is sex and intimacy. But sex is from the first brain, and this is the first brain that you need to go through. A couple came to us complaining of an unfulfilled relationship with no trust, no communication, and no pleasure. When we asked them what they meant by no communication, we found out that actually their ability to listen to each other was very good and their ability to help each other was also very good. We couldn't understand why they were, but our experience has taught us that often people complain about the wrong issue. The real problem is actually so buried that they can't identify it. The main confusion was in a lack of understanding the process of intimacy. When we asked "what is intimacy," they were quite disorganized. He saw intimacy in the relationship through his parents. Intimacy for a man usually ends with sex. When we asked "why sex," he said that his father told him sex can solve anything. With the wife, it was the opposite. She was frustrated that every argument with him was about a need for sex. As a result, she connected sex to anger.

When we checked how they processed their thoughts, we discovered that with her, sex was to please someone, to prevent anger, to solve a crisis. To her, sex was a heavy burden. With him, however, dealing with issues of anger through sex was constructive because he learned from his father that sex solved all problems in a marriage. Once we understood their thought process, we were able to determine that she believed reducing the frequency of sex reduced the amount of bitterness and anger in her marriage. He believed just the opposite. When we separated sex and arguments, we got them to the right place. Sex is a primary problem for many of couples. This couple trusted and loved each other very much and as soon as they were able to find the root of their problem, they could then begin building the ultimate relationship.

Several years ago, a couple came to us with a target to help them build their business. She was an independent contractor, and he was salaried. Out of the conversation, we found that he had a good idea of how her business should look. She had a picture of how her business should look too. She wanted to build a family, and he wanted a big business with a lot of workers for her. He thought she wanted a big business, but she wanted a small business with a family. It was the first time they told each other what they really wanted. He never really listened to what she wanted. He had his own dream and was working to build his dream through her. She was terrified of it. He understood through the conversations that he needed to develop his own business and build his dream, not hers. When they understood each other's dreams, instead of pushing her in the opposite direction, they started to pull each other to the direction they wanted to be. They created cooperation and communication, and they are very happy in their marriage.

A frustrated woman who came to us, married the second time for one year, told us that everything was fine until one day the relationship changed. In her experience, she had a memory about her first marriage that was a lack of trust that developed into jealousy. In her second marriage, because she didn't solve the trust issue and didn't learn her belief system, she rocked the boat before there even was a storm. Her first relationship was a mirror of her parents' relationship. There was infidelity and jealousy, and she reflected it on her first husband, who reminded her very much of her father. We taught her to trust herself and believe in herself before she asks it of another person, especially her husband. We taught her to break the cycle. In order to break the cycle, you have to be aware of the situation and have the will power to change the perception. The ability she was developing to believe in herself didn't allow doubt to get into the relationship, and her marriage was saved.

A man came to us in his late fifties; he didn't know what unconditional love was. Growing up, he hated his parents and didn't feel like he got motherly love. He sought love in other places. In his relationship with women, he gave them material love, physical love, and emotional love in a certain way. He thought they were not giving back the same amount, he felt burned, and he ran away. He said he's like a butterfly looking for warmth that looked too close to the sun and got burned. The emotional feeling he was in was very bad; he was insecure about finding the ideal match for himself. We taught him to forgive, to forgive himself, to forgive his parents for who they are. It was pretty tough procedure for him, connecting him to a feeling of unconditional love that started with his children and then toward the woman that was the ideal woman for him that he found after we finished our discussions.

At a certain stage in marriage it's clear that the winning point gets us nowhere and loses its attractiveness, but on one hand, they are both afraid to rock the boat and on the other end, there is no better solution. So what's next? *This is actually the point of which we are moving up to a higher level of awareness.*

CHAPTER 4 SUMMARY

The three brains correlate with three doors through our daily behavior.

- ✓ Door number one (reptile) – prepare yourself to fit the info you provide to your spouse through the five senses – create a positive impact on the reptile brain and "keep it happy."

- ✓ Door number two (limbic) – emotional control – build up your attitude, decide on your daily being (I'm a loving, giving, supporting person – choose one or more).

- ✓ Door number three (cortex) – awareness and control, be here and now – create optimistic moments at the present with the one you love. Everything I do now creates my past memories, present feeling, and future results.

CHAPTER 4 EXERCISE

When you find yourself frustrated with your spouse and marriage, repeat the three affirmations we teach our clients and soon you'll find that you're calmer and more willing to accept your partner with an open mind.

*"I take full responsibility for myself and
I release the responsibility of others to
provide me with something."*

"I release so things will come easily."

*"I'm present here and now so I'm
projecting the love I have for myself and
attract a partner to this feeling."*

CHAPTER 5
MENTAL INTIMACY

"The best and most beautiful things in the world cannot be seen or even touched. They must be felt with the heart".

—Helen Keller

CHAPTER 5

Your relationship may have started with a physical attraction, but what keeps it strong and fulfilled is a mental attraction. In the first few chapters, you learned how thoughts and paradigms control marriages. For the majority of couples, this filters into their sexual relationships as well. Foreplay isn't just for the bedroom. It is also for our mind. If we truly know our lover and create a third mind, we're able to reach a level of intimacy that no amount of sex can bring. A common theme throughout this book is: think more and do less, and to do so we have to exercise our mental muscles and allow our thinking to determine our results in our relationship.

Our mental muscles are also known as our intellectual faculties. Using these faculties is the only way to raise our awareness. The majority of people's thoughts start to attach to them as soon as they wake up in the morning. All sorts of thoughts bombard us, both good and bad. We automatically hone in on the bad thoughts, which is why it is so important to focus on the positive thoughts. The six intellectual faculties we've been referring to are:

- Reason. Your ability to think and find solutions to all in life.

- Memory. Your ability to help you remember everything you choose to.

- Perception. Your ability to view situations and events from different points of view.

- Will. Your ability to concentrate and focus.

- Intuition. Your ability to listen to other people's feelings (some refer to it as the little voice or internal instinct).

- Imagination. Your ability to create; the key _to the solution of all your problems_

We can use these to originate ideas and infuse intimacy into your relationship. In the next section we're going to explain each one individually, and as you read and learn about them, realize that these mental muscles are extremely powerful once you decide to apply them to your marriage both in and out of the bedroom.

REASON

Reason is our ability to think, to use logic, to gather information, and to make decisions. Our reasoning factor is what helps us determine if a thought is good or bad. We need to use the faculty of reason to choose the thoughts that will make us feel good about ourselves. If we have any negative thoughts about ourselves or our spouse, for that matter, we need to release them. One of the primary reasons so many couples have a great relationship is because they have common goals and focus only on the thoughts that help them achieve those goals. All of the events and situations between the two of you guide your thoughts, feelings, and actions. The faculty of reason is like a recycling bin. It sifts, filters, connects, and organizes all of your thoughts and allows you to throw away any thought that no longer serves you before it enters your subconscious mind. Without that filter all sorts of negative ideas and paradigms flow unobstructed into your subconscious mind. The lack of reason is why so many marriages are on autopilot. Without a thorough understanding of reason, most couples live in the mass level of awareness. They accept their thoughts, words, and actions and just follow along thinking that this is how all marriages are and don't question if this is really if this relationship serves a higher purpose. One couple we coached constantly compared their marriage to their friends'. They mistakenly thought that since their marriage didn't look like everyone else's they knew they weren't in a good relationship. You need to realize that what works for one couple may be the worst solution for another. It's very important to consciously choose what fits best for us in our lives and not just rely on what everyone else is doing.

MEMORY

Memory is our ability to store and recall past experiences. How many times have you forgotten to do something your partner asked of you, such as empty the garbage? As a result you hear some sort of retort as "you have the worst Memory" or "you can't remember anything." Deep in your subconscious mind, you knew you were supposed to do something, but because you didn't make an association, or an X marks the spot on the map of your mind, you forgot to take out the trash.

Most people live with the false impression they have a poor memory. We all have perfect memories; they are just weak and need to be exercised, just as with any other muscle in our body. So how do you strengthen this mental muscle? Create an association. The next time your partner asks you to take out the trash, set your cell phone on the counter above the trash bin. This association is like an information inventory road map that will lead you where everything is stored. When you feel like your mind is going soft and you can't remember anything, it's not your actual memory that breaks down. Your memory is perfect. It's just the retrieval system that needs some work.

Hold that memory on the screen of you mind and close your eyes and focus on all the details. Remember the way it looked, smelled, and felt. Use all your senses and make it feel like you are there in that moment right now. This process stirs your emotional mind. You generate emotions, which will then impact your actions toward your partner. These emotions are going to have an impact on your actions throughout the rest of the day. Our attitude determines our results. Attitude is the energy leaving our bodies. The only method to develop memory is exercise. You have to just do it. Make it a part of your daily life. How many opportunities do we have to practice this in daily life? How often have you misplaced your keys, how often has your partner misplaced his cell phone? With practice and repetition, your answer to these questions will soon be none.

PERCEPTION

Perception is the ability to see with our eyes and not through our eyes. It means being able to see the truth without any interpretation. One couple came to us experiencing difficulty with perception. He wanted to buy a new car and she didn't. He wanted to buy a new car because he's a constructor and he thinks as a constructor he needs an expensive SUV. She did not want to go into debt with a car loan. She perceived the car as an unnecessary expense that will only cause them to have debt. He perceived the need for a car for business. We tried to help them clear up the perception issue about the car. Our first question was to the both of them: what do they agree upon? After we worked with them, the wife realized that her perception of the car bringing debt to their lives was wrong.

They both agreed they need a car for the business, but the argument then became what kind of car to buy. Because he's contractor, he believed he needed a very expensive SUV since in his opinion if he looks successful people will hire him to build their home. In her opinion, the SUV wasn't necessary because it would cost too much, and a moderately priced car would be just fine. When we asked him what other reasons he needed an SUV, he told us most of his work is off road and he needs an SUV to get there. She agreed with him, so they both agreed they needed an SUV. She didn't realize that the majority of his work was not on paved roads, so her perception changed. He also said the SUV would allow him to drive the tools and machinery into the area without hiring a transportation company. This was another aspect she had not realized. His reasons for needing an SUV gave her an understanding so the two of them came to a solution. She changed her perception to the idea that they new SUV would help bring in more income. Seeing through the eyes of our partners rather than just with our own eyes helps us to see the bigger picture of the relationship.

WILL

Will is the ability to focus on a thought or idea while holding out all other distractions. It is the mental faculty that helps us correspond with the world through physical action. Through concentration of focus, we are able to bring about amazing shifts in our relationship. Will allows us to move forward to achieve ideas or goals we set. An important aspect of will is that you can't force something to happen. With will, you must focus, not force. Force negates anything you want to accomplish. In other words, when you are trying to make something happen by your stubborn willpower, you are actually being counterproductive.

Many couples believe that will power is "making" something happen by stubbornness and forcing your desired outcome on the other person. Have you ever tried to force your spouse to change? You may a bit as a result, but before you know it they're back to their old habits. Force is just not a lasting and effective way to get things done. All concentration with the intent of force rather than will distracts us and decreases our ability to focus our concentration on a goal or idea. We live in an age of constant stimulation. All day every day we have information coming at us rapidly through all our five senses; through sights, smells, sounds, touch, and tastes. We spend most of our days on information overload. We have to make time for each other, and couples who have never taken the time to focus on their relationship fall victim to distractions. As we concentrate upon our desired result, the good it will unfold before our very eyes.

Develop the will to ignore what you don't want so you can focus on what you do want. Will empowers you and your spouse to create the relationship you want. The stickperson is a good tool to help us understand how will works. This image represents the screen of your mind with an image on it that has been "paused." Think of will in terms of a screensaver preventing an image from being burnt into your screen while you're away. In the same way, will holds an image on the screen of the mind. Think of your current relationship and an image you want to "burn" onto the screen of your mind and then "pause" it and hold it there until it is firmly impressed upon the subconscious mind. Remember, a thought mixed with emotion is what changes your actions, which changes your results.

Using will is how we get ourselves to move into the direction we want to move. Developing will is essential for us in enabling us to direct our efforts in the direction we want to move—not the direction our paradigms want us to move, but the direction we consciously choose.

INTUITION

Over the years we develop the ability to feel what our spouse or partner is feeling. We need to be able to listen through intuition. One of the best ways to listen through intuition is by listening through emotions. Our spouse's emotions tell us exactly what we need to know and are never wrong. Words don't always convey the right message, while emotions can't hide our true feelings. A woman came to us and complained about her partner, that the things he said to her made her angry. When we asked her what he feels to her, she said love. We asked, "Now, when you think about the things he said with the feeling of love, how do you really feel?" Now she could understand that the things he said were not so bad after all. It doesn't mean that you cannot be angry at each other, it just means that you can forgive.

Have you ever had a hunch or a gut feeling about something? Have you ever walked into a room and just known that something isn't quite right? Our intuition is like an antenna sending us information from another world. Most often your intuition will communicate with you in a small, quiet way. Sadly, few listen to that voice of infinite knowledge and wisdom. Why do we ignore such a valuable counselor and guide in our lives? At best, as we are growing up, we are taught to ignore our intuition—at worst, we are taught to completely distrust it. We will often use our reasoning faculty to discount the hunches or inspiration we receive through our intuition because the ideas don't seem to be "reasonable." We make a decisions based on what we see instead of what we feel.

We allow our faculty of reason to determine that intuition cannot be detected with our five senses; therefore it must not exist. Intuition, however, gives us information we couldn't possibly know using our five senses. There is so much more to the world and universe than we can see with our physical senses! Intuition connects us with the spiritual realm, with God. When we refuse to see the world beyond our physical senses, we are putting a very low ceiling on possibility for growth and knowledge in our lives. It is extremely limiting to disregard such a powerful capacity that is within every one of us.

Just because we can't see it doesn't mean it doesn't exist. We greatly limit ourselves when we only accept the things outside of us. Our real power is within us. Our intuition is the tool we can use to tap into information that surrounds us that exists on a vibrational level that we can't see with our physical eyes. We can't see the hunches or intuitive nudges. We can't see the impression we get that tells us to call a friend we haven't spoken with for a while. We can't see the nudge that tells us to take a different route home because of a car accident. We can't see the foreboding feelings that prompt that something is not quite right. Yet, deep inside we can feel all of these things. We must begin to recognize that our spiritual factors are every bit as real as our sensory factors.

Intuition is similar to a radio, in that if you don't have the radio turned on or if the volume is turned all the way down, you won't be able to hear the messages being received by the radio. You can turn that dial all you want and still not be able to hear a thing. The radio still exists, and it isn't broken; you just don't have it set up properly to receive the transmission. The same applies with your intuition. You must be able to "tune in" to the right station, quiet your reason, and turn the volume up so you can hear the message.

As we listen to its voice, it will speak to us more frequently. If we ignore it, it will stop speaking to us until we are ready to listen. We must learn to trust our intuition completely and act on it. When we stop to analyze and see if an intuitive nudge makes sense with our other faculties, we often skew or warp the intended message. Intuition is always perfect. Our ability to receive and interpret it often is not. Through practice we can improve this ability.

The first step to developing your intuition is to practice being quiet. Turn down all the noises that surround you, including your own thoughts. Silence may be a little uncomfortable at first, but that is just because you aren't used to it. It is vitally important that we provide quiet time for each other. This allows us time to process all the happenings in our relationship.

After you've learned to be quiet, start the practice of intuition with each other's actions. See if you can finish each other's sentences. One of the best ways to start developing a relationship with our intuition is to listen to those nudges and then act on them right away. If you feel like your spouse doesn't feel well, ask her. If you feel like you should check on your partner, go check. Don't discount those feelings. Intuition speaks to you, and you have to be able to hear it. At first, some of your hunches may be strange or wrong. Act on them anyway. By doing so, you're practicing your listening skills. As you get better at hearing the small nudges, you will be ready to hear the important messages as well. Use this as an opportunity to talk to your spouse about what you are doing. When you sense she's had a bad day, ask her about it. Tell her what you're doing and why. As a couple, the two of you observe each move and every word, so a quick discussion when you act on your intuition and whether or not it was right makes a lasting impression.

Trust your intuition and recognize what is going on within to help make decisions in your relationship. Each of you won't have to seek outside approval of what you should do; you will be able to turn inside and find out what is best for you both in that situation.

IMAGINATION

Imagination allows us to see our future. Our imagination is our most important mental faculty that we have because it allows us to see and focus on what we want most in the relationship. It is really wonderful to wake up in the morning and imagine all the wonderful things you want to talk to your spouse about and all the exciting activities you want to do with your spouse to make your relationship even more beautiful. For your ultimate relationship, see your desire in your mind by using your imagination; believe you can have it, and soon it occurs. With our imaginations tucked away, our relationship becomes stagnant. Think about how a little creativity can spice up your own marriage. Imagination is what makes the impossible possible. Without this mental faculty, where we used to say "I can" to any obstacle in our path, we begin to say "I can't."

THEY ARE ALL CONNECTED

We have been conditioned to only use our intellect, which is operating only 10 percent of what runs our daily lives. You see, most of what runs our day-to-day operations is unconscious. This isn't the case when we operate beyond the five senses by using our intellectual faculties. Because our intellectual faculties are related, strengthening one benefits another. We can imagine a happy loving relationship, but why doesn't it happen? Simple. Because reason creeps in and tells us it isn't possible. Some may reason that marriage isn't for them because they grew up with divorced parents, while others may not think they are worthy of love.

Now, instead of focusing on what is "wrong" it is time to use your intellectual faculties and learn how to get the relationship of your dreams. As long as you stay focused on fear and what is wrong, your brain will help you to stay there. You see, what you focus on expands, and what you resist persists.

Your "reality" will show up based on your paradigms. Intuition, for instance, will bring you creative ideas and wisdom for operating your relationships, lead to opportunities, and guide you in ways that the intellect cannot.

To be a whole, empowered couple, you must first be willing to open your mind to new information that will allow you to pull the pieces together in a way that enables you to let go of stories that hold you back and use the new information and paradigms we've read about. You need to integrate all of the intellectual faculties into your daily life.

We need to listen to that inner voice and let it guide us. It has been said that intuition is God's way of speaking to us. When developing your intuition, for instance, using will can be highly beneficial. As we strengthen will, we increase our ability to quiet our minds and focus on receiving messages from that still, small voice. Gandhi uses a beautiful description of how our intuition speaks to us. He says that each of us has this little voice within us, and it speaks to us only as loud as we are willing to listen.

There is a skill in being able to listen to your intuition and not drowning it out with your faculty of reason. We must learn to trust our intuition completely and act on it. When we stop to analyze and see if an intuitive nudge makes sense with our other faculties, we often skew or warp the intended message. Intuition is always perfect. Our ability to receive and interpret it often is not. Through practice we can improve this ability.

If all concentration is done with the will, what would decrease our ability to focus our concentration on a goal or idea? Perception. Most couples second-guess themselves. We want to have this great relationship, but perception moves in and tells us that it isn't possible. Maybe your perception is telling you that you can't be happy because you see and hear so many negative comments about marriage.

Without being able to harness our will and focus it, our power is scattered and ineffective. When we are able to focus our will, it concentrates our energy and allows us to do amazing things, the same way a laser focuses energy into a force that will cut through steel. Without that power of focus we may accomplish a great deal of little things, but very few great things.

Think about your relationship for a moment. Remember some goal that you both set and achieved, or something you both really wanted and got. Once you two decided you wanted that something, what did you both do to go and get it? Whether you were conscious of what you were doing to achieve your desire or not, there is a general process that applies.

Step 1: You listened to that little voice telling you your pattern could needed something more in the relationship. (Intuition)

Step 2: You both dreamed of a goal you wanted to be / do / have. (Imagination)

Step 3: You kept the image of what you wanted in your mind. (Will)

Step 4: You didn't let anyone tell you that your goal wasn't possible. (Perception)

Step 5: You ignored all the negative thoughts telling you that your goal wasn't possible. (Reason)

Step 6. You remember the happiness that the goal brought to your relationship and hold onto that memory when conflict is on the horizon. (Memory)

Without realizing it, we build walls around our mind and our relationship. Remember when you first met; you thought anything was possible, and you had dreams and desires. Remember, the sub-conscious mind does not know the difference between what's real and what is imagined. Build an image of the ideal relationship and live as though it is real—and it will become reality.

To achieve your ideal relationship, the six intellectual faculties are your greatest asset. Individually, they are powerful in their own right, but when used in conjunction with one another you can accomplish any type of marriage you want. Live your ideal (an idea you've fallen in love with); be your ideal and you *will* see your ideal relationship.

CHAPTER 5 SUMMARY

The six intellectual faculties necessary to keep us mentally attracted to our partner include:

- ✓ Reason. Reason allows us to sensibly determine our destination as a couple long before any adverse opportunities present themselves causing us to make a decision in the heat of the moment.

- ✓ Memory. Memory is our ability to store and recall past experiences. Most people live with the false impression they have a poor memory. We all have perfect memories; they are just weak and need to be exercised, just as with any other muscle in our body.

- ✓ Perception. Perception helps us sort out the information coming through our five senses of sight, hearing, smell, taste, and touch. When we change the way we look at our spouse, the spouse we are looking at changes.

- ✓ Will. Will allows us to move forward to achieve ideas or goals we set. An important aspect of will is that you can't force something to happen. We have to focus on a goal or desired outcome, not force it to happen. We must focus, not force.

- ✓ Intuition. Intuition connects us with the spiritual realm, with God, and allows us to see the world beyond our physical senses.

- ✓ Imagination. Everything is created twice—first in our mind, then in reality.

CHAPTER 5 EXERCISE

Choose a goal that you want to achieve in 30 days such as:

- A friendly and loving relationship.

- A wonderful relationship with your spouse

Choose 3 measurable actions that you will do in the next 48 hours that will get you to your goal (setting a date with your spouse, giving compliments, etc…)

CHAPTER 6
THE LAWS OF MARRIAGE

"Like good wine, marriage gets better with age - once you learn to keep a cork in it".

—GENE PERRET

CHAPTER 6

All relationships ebb and flow. You're happy one day and unhappy the next. Every relationship has a reason and a purpose for being created. Finding the reason releases the relationship's potential and takes you toward fulfillment. When you find the cause of your relationship you find that you are not vulnerable to the consequences or thoughts and feelings of your partner. Don't get us wrong; we are not suggesting you stop worrying or relating to others and focus only on yourself—we mean that in order to get a peaceful relationship, you have to accept responsibility for your own emotions. When you are capable of doing this, you are free of stress.

When was the last time you opened your eyes in the sensation of expectation and maybe even excitement over the thought that you were going to spend another day with your partner, or spouse? Is it a day a week, a month, a period? If you haven't felt this sensation of wonder and expectation since in a long time, unfortunately you are not alone. Every marriage needs a solid foundation, and it is important to take great care in properly establishing that foundation because it determines whether or not your relationship is a success. Thus far, we've given you some tools critical for building up your relationship, and now we'd like to add one more to help anchor the two of you. Just as releasing paradigms, learning to use your mental faculties, and increasing your awareness provides a strong and stable relationship, there are precise laws that cement your bond, creating harmony between you and your significant other.

MOVE YOUR RELATIONSHIP TO THE HIGHEST LEVEL

There are universal laws that at first may seem complicated, but remember that it is the application of these laws that is the key to moving your relationship to the highest possible level. When you live according to them, they give you freedom, peace, love, self acceptance, and the ability to give those to your spouse or partner as well. As you read this section, think about how the laws work with or against you and your relationship as you go about your normal daily tasks. Let's discuss each one individually.

The law of attraction states that like attracts like. You attract the thoughts you focus upon. As you are thinking, you are giving energy to the thoughts, and you create a positive or negative vibration throughout your relationship. You create your own reality. We have a very nice story about a girl we know who decided to change her life and activate the law of attraction to find her dream guy. Within two weeks she found him, married him, and they now have two children. She is very happily married because she attracted someone with the same mindset.

We attract the energies that are similar to our own thoughts. Our relationships have been shaped by what we have attracted over the years. For instance, a woman who has the belief that men always treat her badly will continue to attract men who always treat her with disrespect. A man, on the other hand, who believes that women always lie will attract a dishonest mate. Once you are aware of this, you can determine a new course for your life if you do not like your current circumstances. We've coached several couples whose marriage has been improved once they gained a greater understanding of how much of their results have been caused by their own thinking.

It has been interesting for us when we teach this law to our clients because they want to blame each other for their problems. It has taken a lot of time and repetition to undo their thought process, for them to take responsibility for their actions and thoughts about the relationship. Whatever you want in your life you must focus on intently. By focusing on a healthy relationship, you open your mind to the reality of this coming true. Make a conscious decision to examine your thoughts and you'll notice a correlation between them and your relationship.

The law of gender manifests in all things as feminine and masculine energy. You may have heard this as the yin and yang. Both the male and female are required for life to exist. The law of gender, or gestation as it is sometimes called, states that all ideas have a gestation or incubation period before they manifest. So when you set an intention and it doesn't happen automatically, realize that this is the law of gender at work. Be patient, things happen when they are supposed to. You wouldn't plant an acorn and wake up the next morning expecting to see a giant oak tree, would you? No. Well, the same is true with relationships. They take time to nurture and grow. We got married very, very young and found out that we could not get pregnant. It took us five years to solve the problem and get pregnant. When we look back at that experience, we realize that those five years gave us time to build our marriage and get to know each other so we could become good parents and have a happy family. Sometimes you see families in a rush to have a child before they've even based a marriage, hoping the child will glue the marriage. This is the wrong thing to do because, like we say, when you resist nature's laws, you pay the price.

One of the areas that help a marriage grow is a mutual vision and goals. It is so easy for couples to get frustrated because they haven't reached a financial goal or been able to have children. Sometimes the goals we set as a couple don't come to fruition as quickly as we want. This is nothing more than the law of gender working. Like our example above, maybe the fact that you don't have any children yet is the universe's way of telling you your marriage isn't strong enough to handle the added stress of a family. The law of gender is one of the most difficult laws for us to teach our clients. Let's face it: when we want something we want it right now, especially in the age of instant gratification with the internet. Remember, though, if you are living it, if you are talking about it, if you are holding onto your goals, they will happen when they're supposed to. How many times have you ever said to your spouse, "Aren't we glad that this didn't happen back when we thought it should have because look how it would have affected everything else?"

No one knows exactly how long their gestation period is, but be patient! Know that all ideas become a physical reality at the right time. Each goal has a given gestation period, and if you continue to nurture your goals by visualizing them with emotion and by taking action toward them, they will manifest.

The Law of Perpetual Transmutation. Transmutation means changing form, and with this law, we learn that energy moves into physical form. Everything is in constant motion, and that motion is always changing. Energy cannot be created or destroyed. Instead, it is just moved from one form to another. Your thoughts and feelings are the keys to determining what you attract into your life. A couple we met in our seminar decided they wanted to adopt a child, but unfortunately they needed $100,000 to do it. They thought about that amount of money and started preparation to get a loan from the bank. Suddenly, the wife's aunt, who didn't know about the situation, called them and told them that she decided to bequeath them $100,000 while she was still alive. Like all other forms of energy, your thoughts manifest themselves in the physical world. In other words, what you think about you bring about. Just as the couple manifested the money to adopt a child, everything you want or desire moves from your mental thoughts into the physical manifestation of those thoughts, depending on how strongly you believe they will come to be.

The ideas that you are holding in your mind are going to happen with the law of perpetual transmutation. Our thoughts are powerful forces, and it is just as easy to dream big as it is to dream small. Through focused thought, our relationships can be all that we've ever dreamed of. They're energy emitting a vibration and activating the manifestation process according to the law of perpetual transmutation. We literally think things into existence by our thoughts. Thoughts become ideas, and as you accept those ideas, emotions are triggered and expressed with and through the body. Remember, think more and do less. This is so true with this law because once you place your intention and focus your energy toward it, the body acts accordingly.

The Law of Relativity. All things are relative. Everything in life just "is," and it's only by comparison that it becomes something else. The way we perceive our relationship is always relative to how we see another couple interact. Couples who think that other couples have a better relationship need to understand this law. You cannot compare your relationship to a very good one because there is always going to be a relationship worse than the one you are currently in. So in order to look at that law you need to see only what there is, the reality, and in the reality there is no bad or good, it's what it is. This is a great law to strengthen your marriage because it allows us to gauge what we see. Is someone's relationship better or worse than ours? It depends on whose we're comparing to ours. Because of this, no matter where you are in life, there are numerous things to be grateful for now, while you work toward what you want. Stop comparing your relationship to others and just accept and love each other for who you are. No marriage or relationship is better or worse, they are just different.

Don't dwell on how your situations are not as good as someone else's. What we are doing as couples is giving each other points of reference by which we compare everything. We can't judge whether something is good or bad in our life by our reactions to things. When something happens in our relationship, we place a judgment on it based on what our parents have taught us and programmed us to believe. Whether it is what is good and what is bad, what is scary and what is not scary, what is fun and what is boring. Those are all things programmed by our parents, and we make a judgment in our own relationship in our own mind based on those programs.

Once we become aware of this law we can focus on our relationship and no one else's. Our perception is what shapes our marriage into what we see and experience. As we are able to change our perception, it changes the world that you see around you. **Sometimes in our life we think that when something bad happens, it is punishment. This is not the case at all. The law of polarity** states that there is a good and bad in everything. You can't have a hot without a cold or an up without a down. For every argument, there is a lesson to learn. Everything bad that happens has something good inside. For instance, when

Ossi's mother passed away, it was of course a very bad thing, but when looking at it from a distance, it's what pushed her to change her career, so her whole vision of life changed.

The problem is that most couples focus on the negative aspect of events. Instead, you must look for the good in every event because there is always something good hidden in a bad situation. We have to keep our minds focused on the positive at all times, which makes all the difference. The law of polarity gives us an opportunity to pause and think about every occurrence that we have in our marriage. When something happens, we have a choice to look at it as a good event or a bad situation. As humans, we seem drawn to find the bad in everything. Unfortunately, most people don't take the next step and look for the good in the situation.

You need to take every bad event that occurs in your relationship and tell yourself that there is something good that is to come of this. Then, actively look for the lesson or good situation that comes as a result of the bad. We have the privilege of interpretation, so we can choose to view any situation as a positive or a negative. From that choice, we set vibration in motion, our vibration determines our feelings, and our feelings drive our actions and results. Find that seed of equivalent benefit in every situation, and the good results will follow. Train your mind to be aware that in life both good and bad exist and there is always a lesson to be learned from the bad.

Everything in the universe moves in a repetitive rhythm. Tides rise and fall, the sun sets and rises. For every action there is an action, which is all established by **the law of rhythm.** These patterns in life help to balance us. Our relationships are no different. There are ups and downs, and we have to understand that for all downs, there are ups and vice versa.

Relationships have rhythm of their own, and we want to think to this rhythm. Otherwise we are fighting. By understanding that all marriages operate according to the law of rhythm, it is possible to prevent problems or arguments. So if you are building a relationship, the flow will not sink you and the low will not dry you.

It is important to realize that we aren't going to feel in love all of the time; no one does. If we did, would we even know when we were happy? The valleys allow us to enjoy the peaks in our lives. It is important for us to remember that even when we are on a natural down swing we can choose positive and encouraging thoughts. When you realize that you are feeling ill will toward your partner, consciously begin thinking about something good. If you have a setback on your way toward a good thought, stop, visualize, and feel yourself as you will be when you reach your good emotional state.

Switch your brain into positive thought mode. We realize that when you want to put an ax through your partner's head, it is extremely difficult to think positive thoughts. However, even if you only take a short amount of time, say 20 seconds, when you begin to think of something positive you will move your vibration to a more positive state. This small increase will help bring to you other positive thoughts, which in turn take you to an even higher level. Through the repetitive nature of thinking positive thoughts, even in small increments, you will continue to move to higher and higher levels of vibration, and you will work your way back into the feeling of love toward your spouse and put the ax back in the tool shed.

When you learn to notice when you are in a negative state and can change your thoughts and work yourself to a happier state, you will feel empowered and have control over your emotions and respond instead of react. If you find yourself in a downward swing, know that it's part of the rhythmic cycle and there are good times coming, visualize them, and raise your vibration.

Sir Isaac Newton said every action has a reaction, equal and opposite. Every cause has an effect; every effect, a cause—no exceptions. Our actions have consequences. So the principle of **the law of cause and effect** relates to everything, including our thoughts. Every thought we create has a certain wavelength, and it does not occur randomly. All our thoughts occur for a specific purpose. Thoughts are a reflection of our way of thinking and how we feel about ourselves and our relationship. Many people struggle with this principle because it forces them to take responsibility. It means that we cannot blame other people or other circumstances for anything that happens in our life. We have the ability to create the event and the circumstances in our life. When we don't recognize this principle in our life and take action in our life it's easy for us to relate to ourselves as the reaction of all of those events instead of seeing that we are the cause of the event. We start to believe that things just happen to us, and it leads us to a mentality of being a victim.

Unfortunately, most couples either aren't aware that everything is energy and its relation to the universal laws or don't take the time or put forth the effort to develop an awareness of how to align their marriage with these laws. However, if they would live according to these laws they would, with exact certainty, give their relationship the tools to succeed. Instead, most couples try to create happiness through spending more money on each other and giving each other more material possessions. This is only a temporary solution. Several of our clients who have the happiest and most fulfilling marriages live according to the universal laws. They understand and apply them daily.

Discover your true power now by acting in accordance and in harmony with the universal laws. Trust your marriage to the laws, not your paradigms. Couples who live according to these laws are in harmony. To help our clients better understand the relationship of these laws to their marriage we tell them to say them out loud when they apply to certain situations or events. If you identify and learn them for what you are experiencing or what you are identifying, down the road it can be just, "Hey, honey…rhythm" and a potential argument has just been avoided.

A firm understanding of these laws is a distinguishing factor for happy and unhappy relationships and learning to align with these laws will lead your marriage down a path filled with hope, abundance, happiness, joy, fulfillment, and peace. When couples discover that there is an order to the universe and that certain laws govern it, they can then use this knowledge to master any area of their relationship they want. The fundamental laws enable us to meet the challenges of life with confidence. These universal laws are at work 100 percent of the time regardless of your awareness or ignorance of them. Your thoughtful, conscious choice is the only thing that determines how they work and what is created for you.

CHAPTER 6 SUMMARY

The Laws of Marriage:

- ✓ Every marriage needs a solid foundation, and it is important to take great care in properly establishing that foundation because it determines whether or not your relationship is a success.

- ✓ There are universal laws that if understood and applied will move your relationship to the highest possible level.

- ✓ The law of attraction states that like attracts like.

- ✓ The law of gender manifests in all things as feminine and masculine energy. All ideas have a gestation or incubation period before they manifest.

- ✓ The law of perpetual transmutation states that everything is in constant motion and that motion is always changing.

- ✓ The law of relativity states that everything in life just "is," and it's only by comparison that it becomes something else.

- ✓ The law of polarity states that there is a good and bad in everything.

- ✓ The law of rhythm states that everything in the universe moves in a repetitive rhythm.

- ✓ The law of cause and effect states that every action has a reaction, equal and opposite.

CHAPTER 6 EXERCISE

How familiar were you with the laws of universe and the laws of marriage?

____

____

What can you learn about yourself and how can you act differently?

____

____

Discuss this with someone close to you and share the process that you are going through (it does not have to be your spouse).

CHAPTER 7
STRONG INDIVIDUALS
MAKE STRONG MARRIAGES

*"By all means marry; if you get a good
wife you'll be happy. If you get a bad
one you'll become a philosopher".*

—SOCRATES

CHAPTER 7

Your spouse's opinion of you is oftentimes based upon your own self-image. How you see and think about yourself is your self-image. Your self-image, or your "inner mirror" as it's often referred to, determines how you behave and, consequently, how your relationship is. You are where you are and who you are because of the beliefs you have about yourself. You can have all the positive intentions imaginable, but if you haven't changed your internal picture your relationship more than likely isn't as fulfilling as it can be.

"In the first 10 years of our marriage my self-image was as low as it could get; I was afraid to express myself, I could not say NO to people, I was constantly afraid to say NO to anyone that asked me to. Even though I did not want to, I felt miserable and frustrated; I went to a Dale Carnegie seminar just to learn to say NO. It was my first time on stage, leading me to start believe that I could change." – Ossi

"In the first years of our marriage I felt like I was pushed to take control of every aspect of our joined life. I even felt uncomfortable with Ossi's behavior around people and friends. We argued a lot, me trying unsuccessfully to change her outside behavior, telling her do that or do not was the stupidest thing I've done, believing it would help her." Dan

In your sub-conscious mind you have an image of how much you think you're worth—based on family history, beliefs instilled when growing up, and experiences. And you only vary from that image by a very small percent. If your self-image suggests you're unworthy, who do you think you attract? Sadly you get involved with partners who treat you poorly. How you see, think, and feel about yourself determines what you project to your husband or wife. Are you honest and trustworthy? Does your spouse reflect that back to you? If you want a loving and caring marriage, you have to give it first. Raise your vibration to attract your wants and needs. Before you can reap the harvest you have to plant the seeds and nourish them. Let's take a quick look at self-esteem time frame we share with our clients:

- Age 3: You view yourself as a loved child.

- Age 8: You view yourself as indestructible.

- Age 15: You view yourself as inferior.

- Age 20: You view yourself as "too fat / too thin / too short / too tall / too straight / too curly"—but decide to go out anyway.

- Age 40: You look at yourself and see what could have been.

You can't receive any emotions or feelings that aren't already present within you. Why? Because 95 percent of the drivers that determine where you focus your attention are coming from the sub-conscious mind. We don't see things as they are; instead we see them as we are. Once a person rids himself of his limiting beliefs and releases, he begins to see himself in a different light. For instance, if you don't feel worthy of love and respect, how can you attract that into your marriage? Instead, take an internal inventory and create a paradigm shift. Look at yourself as worthy of love and a great marriage. As soon as you plant the seed and nourish it, you'll be able to attract what you want in your marriage and sustain it for many years to come. This is how the manifestation process works.

So if you don't like what you're seeing around you, ask this question: "What is it that I'm not giving to my spouse or significant other?" Then start to give whatever you're yearning for—get to know and understand what it feels like, and you will attract it. Remember the law of attraction—like attracts like. What you're attracting is a reflection of your inner self. Stop viewing your marriage through your paradigms. Expand your awareness, make a change within, and watch your marriage grow and flourish. Notice how your relationship improves as your self-image improves. As you feel better about yourself, you have so much more to give to others—and it comes back multiplied!

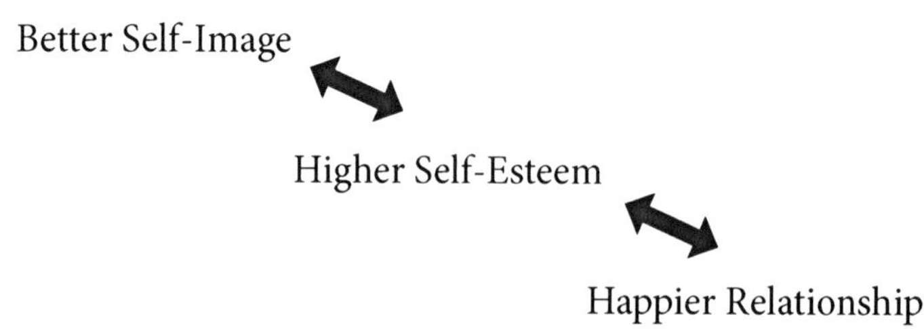

Without a good self-image, you can easily start agreeing with others who try to break you down with harsh criticism. You then tear yourself down, rather than viewing their criticism objectively as an opinion about your behavior rather than a critique of yourself. Confidence is one of the keys to getting what you want in life. In turn, as you get what you want, you feel more confident and have a better self-image. When you don't have a positive self-image, you are a target for other people's perceptions of you, and you can easily get sucked into their belief about you. In turn, that can translate into many negatives, such as not asking for and therefore not getting what you want at work. Then, too, if you don't feel confident about what you are worth, you will evaluate yourself less favorably and will get less—less money, less benefits, less prestige, less power, less of everything in all areas of life.

As the Golden Rule states: "Do unto others as you would have them do unto you." This is paramount in our marriage, and it should be in your relationship to0. For any relationship to be fulfilled, it is imperative to treat your partner in three ways:

- Like to be treated.

- Love as you like to be loved.

- Give as you like to receive.

THE ICING ON THE CAKE

Before we go any further, let us first point out that when we speak of healthy self-esteem, we're not just talking about positive thinking. We use the analogy of icing on a cake when we discuss this concept with couples. A cake may look delicious with creamy icing and decorative flowers and designs, but if it doesn't have any sugar in it, then it won't taste nearly as good as it looks. This is true for us as well. Looking good on the outside doesn't necessarily mean the inside matches. Our outer body might look great, but if it's thriving on bad decisions, destructive habits, and limiting beliefs, the inside is breaking down. Both your external and internal beings have to be in harmony and alignment with your desires. Your thoughts, feelings, and actions must work together. You have to become aware of what is preventing you from having positive self-esteem.

Self-love is the pathway to healthy self-esteem and the key to a fulfilling marriage. It gives you permission to be who you are and to love and accept yourself and others. Remember, self love is non-conditional. Regardless of your past accomplishments, successes, or failures, you have value. Accept all aspects of yourself, even the ones you don't like, and be yourself. Healthy self-esteem is sabotaged by reliving your past. When you travel back in time, feelings of guilt and regret surface in not only your life but in your marriage as well. Remember what's done is done—no matter how hard you try you can't go back in time and change what's happened, but you can release any emotional charges attached to that experience. By dwelling on the past you're only replaying old movies and reliving the experience again, with more intensity. Let it go. Accept it, learn from it, and move on.

The purpose of life is to grow and evolve into the best person you can be, and that includes learning new skills, stepping out of your comfort zone and stretching yourself, taking risks at times and doing things that can greatly improve your lifestyle. What most people believe, however, is that they have to accomplish great feats or have tremendous success in order to have good self-esteem. In reality, it is exactly the opposite. Until you accept your greatness, you'll live a life less than ordinary. Stop focusing on the parts of you that you don't like. How do you feel when you constantly criticize yourself? Our guess is not good. By focusing your attention on what you can't change, you're only magnifying the situation, giving it more energy, and robbing yourself of confidence. When you accept your self-imposed flaws and make the decision to focus on only the good, they lose their power over you and your relationship. Release your needless worries and accept yourself for who you are; besides, most people don't even notice your imperfections, and furthermore, they don't care! They're too busy worrying about themselves! Practice self-love and self-acceptance and remember you are unique and have value. The more you love yourself, the more you're able to love your spouse and the better your relationship will be.

WHO ARE YOU?

There won't be a lasting change in your relationship until you change your self-image. Is there anything about you that strikes a chord? Do you criticize yourself constantly? Are you dissatisfied or unhappy about the way you look? Now is a great time to take an honest look at the picture of you that you're projecting to your partner. What is the continuous movie that's controlling your life? Make the decision to say no to unwanted results and take the time to make a change, to love and accept yourself just as you are. Be grateful for the circumstances and conditions that have brought you to this place.

Can you imagine the difference in your marriage if you began to work on yourself, grow in your level of awareness, and be loved, one step at a time, one challenge at a time? Slowly at first, then faster and faster the collective energy would rise to a new level—a much higher vibration. How magnificent would that look and feel! You choose your path—there are many, and you reach your destination when you believe you can. Sometimes that means being true to yourself and not listening to other people's opinions.

So many people care what others think because they want to be liked and accepted; they want to belong—to be like everyone else. They fear rejection. In order to please others, their own desires are sometimes neglected. After all, "love makes the world go round," doesn't it? What other people think is none of your business Do you try to please your spouse? Do you put their needs in front of your own? Just like the instructions on the airplane say, put your oxygen mask on before your child's; we need to do the same in our marriage. This may sound selfish, but you can't be a good spouse to someone and show love if you don't take care of your own needs.

You are responsible for how you live and who you choose to be. What other people think about your choices is irrelevant. How can anyone possibly know what you want? They're not you! They're only coming from their perspective. Criticism, unwanted advice, and too many opinions can be confusing and destructive, lowering your vibration and diminishing your self-image. If you make decisions based on your own beliefs not those of other people, why do you need confirmation from others? Make an informed decision to either accept or reject it based on what feels true to you. Most importantly for a healthy self-image, love and respect yourself and your opinions. How do you want to be perceived in your marriage? Do you want to project the truth of who you believe you are and to have that truth recognized? Be aware of the messages you're sending and how they're being perceived. You can always change any inconsistencies!

Who is the person you most want to be? This is your self-ideal, your vision of what the perfect person should be in every respect. It largely determines how your relationship will be. We star our life "modeling" someone at a very young age. First it's likely to be our parents, then friends, and as we grow older we may choose to be like the models or film stars we see in glossy magazines, or a pop star. On and on the list goes—a successful entrepreneur or salesperson or a great mother—whoever it is, the person you model has a powerful influence on your behavior and the way you think about yourself.

Throughout your life you've developed values based on what you've observed, what you've experienced, and what you think and feel about qualities like love, confidence, courage, forgiveness, honesty, leadership, and friendship—to name a few. And you do your best to live up to them as you strive to become the best person you can be. To be clear about the person you choose to be. Without clarity you have no direction. You can't hit a target you can't see. Look up to and respect fine qualities in others and incorporate them into your own life—it feels great. You don't have to reinvent the wheel.

Instead, look at your true self and learn as much as you can about your values, beliefs, and strategies. Integrate them into your life; maybe some of them you have already! Act as though you are the person you're choosing to be and celebrate as you notice improvements in every respect—work, relationships, and well-being. Why? Because you're moving to a new level of awareness, and as you change, your conditions, circumstances, and environment change. Now that you're pretty clear on your self-ideal—the person you'd most love to be—do you believe you can be that person?

Now let's take a look at your self-concept. Your self-concept is the composite of your self-image and self-esteem, just as your attitude is the composite of your thoughts, feelings, and actions. All three go hand in hand. Your self-concept is your belief structure, and it controls the decisions you make. It determines the way you think and feel; what you "sort for";

and how you behave. Will you be happily married or divorced? Your beliefs were formed in your childhood and onwards and here's the good news: if they're not serving you, they can be changed! Change your beliefs and you change your world. Your outer world is a reflection of your inner world: as within, so without.

Did you know you also have a self-image around your environment? Look around you—do your neighbors share similar standards and values? What type of car do you think you should drive; which suburb should you live in; how much money do you deserve; where do you like to dine; where do have your holidays and so on. You have an internal picture regarding where to live, who to mix with, and how to behave. Take an honest look at how you react to certain situations, such as your spouse's success. Are you envious, jealous or resentful of him? What negative energy does such a reaction generate, and for what purpose? Your negative vibration resonates with and attracts more negative situations. Is that what you choose? Instead, why not celebrate your spouse's success. That way you're not only raising your own vibration, but your intentions for your partner are much kinder and more supportive too. You only attract people, situations, "things" that resonate with who you are.

Many people compare themselves to others. They judge their worth and success against others—their parents, their siblings, their friends, their work colleagues, or even the rich and famous. Most often their comparisons are against people whom they perceive to be more successful, smarter, better-looking, slimmer, healthier, wealthier, or happier than they are. They don't stop to think about those who are far worse off. And there is always someone worse off because everything in the universe has its equal and opposite (the law of polarity) and everything is relative (the law of relativity). Even your rates of vibration are either high or low when compared with those above or below them. Use the law of relativity to your advantage if you must compare! Everything in life just "is," and it's you who makes it so. You see, the way you see yourself is not who you are but rather who you think you are. What are you attracting?

We have worked with many couples who were able to turn their marriage around and become happy by starting with a change in attitude about themselves. They started off feeling uncertain about who they really were and ended up feeling confident by focusing on their good qualities, seeing themselves as successful, and visualizing themselves as prosperous and recognized by others for their efforts and achievements. One particular couple comes to mind. We met them at one of our seminars; the wife had absolutely no self-esteem. She found it difficult to leave the house most days. We met with her for several weeks, helping her to uncover the limiting beliefs tied to her negative self-image. Once she was able to see the correlation, she made the decision to change her thoughts and created a paradigm shift. She is now happy with herself, and her marriage is fulfilling for both her and her husband.

We teach the philosophy that if you believe you have value, you have value! And you need to start out with that belief; it helps to create the experiences you have that support this belief. Once you develop a firm self-image, you have that "I can do it anything" feeling, and you're ready to take on new responsibilities, which lead to personal growth. If you believe you can do it, you can. It all comes back to belief. You must believe you have the power to create the life you want, and then that belief empowers you to follow through.

The key to improving your self-image is to overcome fears, anxieties, self-doubts, and limiting beliefs, such as "I can't do it" or "I'm not good enough." You have to focus on what you can do, know you can do it, and see yourself doing it. Whenever we think about what we do well, it's a form of self-affirmation that builds our self-image. Remember, it is all about belief. If you believe—you have them, you'll develop them, and your self-image will improve. Self image is basically just about how you feel about yourself. You either like yourself or you don't. If you don't like who you see in the mirror, it is probably difficult to trust yourself, or anyone else for that matter.

Very often people with a poor self image have difficulty identifying their talents and abilities. They don't believe they have anything to offer the world. Was it hard for you to complete your list? Now, we want to teach you how to replace your old beliefs with new positive ones about yourself. You have to affirm what you want to get and truly believe what you affirm. In the space provided below, write down your affirmations about who you are or want to be. Make certain to write your affirmations in the present tense. Remember that even if you don't have that quality now, by truly believing you will become the person you want to be. The qualities must align with the person you want to become in your lifetime.

"A boy came to me with a very low self-image; he had never experienced success, he asked what success looks like. I asked him what success would look like for him. He said that "if I could score a goal in soccer game, it would be a success for me." We practiced the mind imagining a soccer goal-scoring process and how he would feel after. Two days later he called me just to let me know that he did it. Since then, he has become a leader in his class".
–Ossi

Select your most important affirmation and focus on it for about a minute. Now repeat your affirmation over and over to yourself for two to three minutes. As you do this, see the statement you have written in your mind's eye. Don't just hear or see the words but translate your message into a visual image. Practice this technique once a day for the next twenty-one days, and soon you'll notice that you feel better about yourself and that the things you want will start coming into your life.

Affirmations are powerful tools because the process leads to a subtle attitude change that affects the way you feel about yourself by transforming your beliefs. As affirmations build your self-image, adding visualization increases the magnitude of your beliefs. This process works because not only do you make yourself more aware of who you are, but by seeing yourself as successful, healthy, rich, or whatever you want to be in life, in the here and now, you feel what it is like to experience it. You're using mental imagery to convince yourself that you are experiencing what you want in the here and now, and your feelings and actions respond to complement and reinforce that mental image.

By focusing on and visualizing what you want, you will experience life-altering transformations. The following visualization exercise should be repeated once a day for thirty days to reinforce and strengthen your self-image. Later, you can turn these feelings into reality by initiating new actions to implement your vision.

Begin by deciding what you want most out of life. Next, relax, close your eyes, and see yourself realizing this goal. Make your image of this achievement as vivid as possible and see your success happening in the here and now. As you visualize your success, experience the satisfaction and feeling of power this brings. Feel elated, excited, strong, powerful, fully self-confident, and in charge. Then see others coming up to you or calling to congratulate you. You feel warm and glowing as you receive their praise. They tell you how successful you are. And you feel wonderful, able to do anything you want. Affirming and visualizing your abilities and talents and seeing yourself as an abundant, successful person helps you to take full control of your life.

You need to decide the self-image best for you and your own career or business path. Then you can decide if you have the self-image you want or determine the areas you want to develop further to get closer to your worthy ideal. You'll find the results can be amazing if you decide to make some changes—a job more in line with your abilities and interests; improved job performance and a higher income; and more personal power at work and at home.

Determine what you want to become. Ask yourself: "How would I like to change?" However you want to change, the exercises we discussed can help you imagine the qualities you want to eliminate and those you want to develop. Once you decide who you want to be, rehearse the role over and over again in your mind until you reinforce the reality of this new image. So you see yourself differently when you act in the real world, which helps you act differently as well.

Now you take the new role and actions you have created for yourself and put them into practice in real-life situations. The process of creating a new self-image is much like the process of setting and achieving goals. You start off thinking about who you want to become, then decide which qualities are most important to you so that you can work on achieving them first. Then, in turn, you'll bring those qualities into your relationship.

CHAPTER 7 SUMMARY

- ✓ Our self-image determines the way we think, feel, and act.

- ✓ How we see, think, and feel about ourselves determines what we project to our spouse or partner.

- ✓ We can't receive any emotions or feelings that aren't already present within us, and we don't see people, situations, circumstances, or events as they are; instead we see them as we are.

- ✓ Without a good self-image, we can easily start agreeing with others who try to break us down with criticism.

- ✓ Self-love gives us permission to be who we are and to love and accept ourselves and others. Regardless of our past accomplishments, successes, or failures, we all have value. If we believe we have value, we have value!

- ✓ Take the new role and actions you have created for yourself and put them into practice in real-life situations. Whatever you do, do as you are the person you want to be.

- ✓ Choose one value that you would like to have, such as love, sensitivity, or listening, etc. Focus on that value for the next thirty days. Ask yourself how your relationship will look when you're acting this way.

CHAPTER 7 EXERCISE

Below is a short questionnaire about your self-image. Read through each statement and mark it either True or False.

Statement	True	False
I admit my mistakes.		
I stand behind my values even if others disagree with me.		
I accept my faults.		
I love who I am.		
I don't compare myself with others.		
I believe I have something to offer others.		
I don't care what other people think of me.		
I don't change my personality to suit others.		
I am not afraid to list my strengths and abilities.		

If your list consists mainly of the answer True, you have a good self-image. If your list was filled with Falses, you need to take a serious look at the following ways to build your self-image. As you improve your self-image, you will not only feel better, but you'll get much more out of everything you want. You will ask for it, you will feel you deserve it, and other people will agree too. Your attitude will convey that message, and as other people get your message, they can't help but agree as well.

CHAPTER 8
MUTUAL PURPOSE, VISION, AND GOALS

"There's only one way to have a happy marriage and as soon as I learn it I'll get married again".

—Clint Eastwood

CHAPTER 8

A successful marriage is more than a happy family, great children, a nice home and a pleasant intimate life. King Solomon once said "without a vision people perish." Couples have to have a mutual purpose, vision, and set of goals. When we visualize our life together, our shared purpose, vision, and goal are to lecture to an international audience to motivate and inspire couples around the world to follow their dreams. When couples fall into an "is this all there is" feeling, they lack a shared experience with each other. Having a nice married life is just not enough; sharing a mutual journey creates inner fulfillment.

We've all heard of marriages where the spouses seemed to have little or nothing in common, and the marriage survived, but in reality, these are rare cases. Fifty years is a long time to stay together with nothing to say to each other. Couples need a purpose. Boredom can and will set in quickly if the marriage has no common ground, so couples need to nurture their marriage with mutual interests, to give them topics of conversation, if nothing else.

When a couple makes the decision to commit to a long-term relationship, they should do so by looking at the future through the eyes of their spouse. A truly fulfilling marriage begins when a couple comes together and uses their third mind to look through their spouse's eyes to see the same purpose, vision, and goals, which makes it so much more powerful. It may not feel as stable and safe at first because it takes time and planning to learn how to work together, how to move together, and how to trust each other. Supporting each others' individual purpose, vision, and goals are vitally important, but not having a shared purpose, vision, and goals leads to separate lives and a sense of loneliness. Couples need to create a "marriage plan" to define mutual long-term vision and to set the signposts for the smaller steps they need to take to create a shared life.

MARRIAGE ON PURPOSE

Your purpose is the driving force, the burning desire that propels you toward realizing your dreams and achieving your goals. What most people don't realize is that a couple needs a purpose too. What are you and your spouse purposeful about? Many couples struggle to answer this. They simply don't know. Their relationship has become very routine—a mere existence. Yet every marriage has a spark within waiting to be ignited. It's just that most of us have been wearing masks all our lives in the shape of our paradigms. Take off that mask, move beyond your old beliefs, and be the couple you were meant to be.

The purpose of the marriage is the vehicle, and your personal purpose is the fuel that drives it toward your vision and goals. Imagine how your life would look if you were to have a mutual purpose in your marriage.

Are you ready to design your marriage and have the life that you choose? Begin the following self-discovery exercise by directing your sub-conscious mind to reveal your passion as a couple. Expect answers and accept what comes up. It doesn't have to be anything big or newsworthy. It could be as simple as loving the time you spend with your family or time in nature. Answer the question below to find your marriage's purpose. If money was no object and there was absolutely no chance of "failure," what would you and your spouse do each day?

Write it down. Keep writing—every little thing you can think of. Dream big! Your answers to the previous question shed light on the type of couple you are. There's no right or wrong; these questions are for you to understand who you are, so trust your sub-conscious mind and your intuition as the answers come to the surface. You're letting go of the "shoulds" and replacing them with what's important to you and your partner.

When you are living your marriage with purpose and directing your life with purpose you are in control of your life rather than living a life that is controlling you and the events around you, which is just an accident waiting to happen, often with disastrous results. A purpose-driven marriage gives you a life with intention and direction, and every day that goes by you learn who you are, the meaning of life for yourself, and what is truly important for yourself and your family. Your decision-making becomes easier and you see no boundaries. Your values are clear, and overall you are in a happy state because a life that is purpose-driven answers the questions of what the meaning of your marriage is and what the two of you are meant to do as a couple.

> *"Years ago I added into our joint vision that Dan and I work together to help people achieve their ideal lifestyle. I was a life coach and Dan was a corporate CFO at that time. He laughed about it but agreed to keep it. Two years later we formed our company and started working together." –Ossi*

A MUTUAL VISION

Creating a vision is an important part of a successful relationship. Writing a vision statement allows you and your partner to dream, to imagine the life that you would like to live together, and to determine the course of your relationship. It is like drawing a map that you will use on the journey that you are taking towards building a healthy connection.

A successful relationship vision should be aligned with your strengths and core values. Once your vision is created, you can then set very specific goals in order to realize your vision. Your vision might begin with a peaceful evening together. As you work on your vision statement it may grow to include things like remodeling your home to create the dream house you both want or taking a trip to an exotic destination that will satisfy your craving for adventure. The first step to creating this shared vision is to visualize your dream marriage.

Now, both of you dedicate a half hour to discuss what your dream marriage looks like. Have fun with it and really go for it; remember that there are no limitations to what you can dream about. There are no time or money restraints, no past history, and no future worries. Write down only what is mutually agreed upon. Whichever way the paragraph comes out is good; there are no right and wrong answers as long as it represents your joint vision.

There is an incredibly transformative effect just in having a clearly defined vision. A couple once came to me for counseling but left after only one session because the husband decided that he did not want to put in the work. It just was not worth it to him. We happened to do this "dream marriage" exercise in the one session that we shared. I ran into the couple about a year later at a friend's wedding, and we sat down to chat. They told me that a weird thing was happening with their relationship: they were beginning to live their "dream marriage" statement without even trying.

There is a subconscious shift that occurs when you have a dream vision. It is as if you set a new direction for your relationship and then simply have to wait for your life to play it out.

Visions are not carved in stone and will grow and change as you and your partner grow and change. Your vision should reflect important aspects of your life, such as:

- How and when do you want to spend your time together?

- What problem areas do you want to overcome?

- What areas do you want your relationship to grow in?

- What are your hopes and dreams for your family and for your children?

- What are your thoughts about money?

- How do you each think about savings?

- Do you have dreams that need to be included in your financial plans?

Your vision should be exciting and meaningful to each of you. Aspects of the vision should make a difference in your lives, and the results should be something that you can see and can measure. Your vision statement should include dreams for the relationship as well as dreams for each of you individually. This is the time to play. Have fun jotting down the things that you have always wanted for yourself and your relationship. How you will actually bring the vision to life is through the goals that you will put into place.

Too often people get stuck when they think about creating a vision, especially if their relationship feels hopeless and overwhelming. People often worry that their vision may not be important or might be too different from their partner's. It is not uncommon to feel anxious or guilty for wanting something in your life when you have been used to denying yourself. Take your time and create your vision over several days if necessary. Just remember you can't get to your destination without a map!

While it would be ideal to create a vision statement with your partner, you can also do it on your own and invite your partner to listen to the dreams that you have for yourself and your relationship. Find a quiet time when the two of you will be free from distractions to share your vision. Bear in mind that this is a map, not a statement of exactly how things will be. You are dreaming of the possibilities for yourself and your relationship, and the goals that you put into place will be steps in helping you achieve the vision that you dream of.

Your vision (as distinct from your purpose that supports it), is an overall idea perceived vividly in the imagination—a dream with direction. Vision is seeing through the eyes, as opposed to sight, which is seeing with the eyes. Note the distinction. Everyone has a vision, and every marriage needs one too. Your life is the direct result of it; the key is to be happy with what you envision and not to judge by appearances. Appearances only reveal who you used to be—they are a reflection of your past thoughts, feelings, and actions up to this point. They are not who you are! Remember this. You can create a new life right now.

COMBINED GOALS

The purpose of a goal is to set an intention and to activate the law of attraction. Goals also inspire you to make the necessary changes to become the person ready to handle the goal; to be in resonance with the opportunities offered, courtesy of your intuition. If you're vibrating at a lower frequency, you miss the opportunity. Goals raise your level of conscious awareness and improve all areas of your life, not just the specific area of the goal—to go beyond what you already know, to expand your awareness, to stretch the boundaries and grow. A goal gives direction to your sub-conscious mind so that it knows what to sort for. Choose where you're heading in life by your goals and stay focused on them with your attention.

We set goals all the time, either consciously or unconsciously. We either create or disintegrate. What about your thoughts? Are you creating or disintegrating your goals? Goals grow out of the vision that you and your partner create together. They are the milestones that you create in order to reach the final outcome—a healthy, fulfilling relationship. Once your vision is created it is time to break it down into manageable pieces. These are the actions and tasks that will need to be taken in order to reach your final destination.

The goals should be small steps so that you will be successful in reaching each in turn. These steps may be something that you do alone or things that you do as a couple. You are writing a road map that includes the milestones that will help guide you toward your vision for yourself and relationship.

Your goals should be measurable. They can be anything from going out on a date once a week to registering to take classes to making a career changes. You and your partner will create the goals that are meaningful to you both. While learning to eat in a healthier way and exercising three times per week might be a goal for one couple, planning a trip may be a goal for another. You get to create the vision and support it with the goals that suit you and help you develop the trusting, loving relationship that you deserve.

Couples who sit down together and take the time to spell out what their own expectations and desires and hopes are have a high chance of future success and happiness together when they make plans for things they both want. When people come together they bring with them their individual background, family history, and family habits and expectations. If one of you is expecting one thing and the other has a different goal, people can become disappointed and disillusioned. A simple discussion and planning process might overcome potential problems and lead to excitement and fulfillment together.

Write your goals in the different areas in your life, such as:

Lifestyle (which can include your home, environment, and travel)

____

____

____

Body, Soul, Mind (health, education, etc.)

____

____

____

Relationships (family, friends, workmates)

____

____

____

Love, Sex, Romance (intimacy)

____

____

____

Anything you think of that you want

____

____

____

Try the following to make your goals powerful:

- Go within and explore. What do you really want? Want, not need—aim as high as you can. The sub-conscious mind knows no difference between real and imagined; the only prerequisite is that you believe in your ability to achieve your goal—otherwise those negative voices in your head take over and destroy your confidence.

- Dream. If you knew there was no chance of failure, what would you choose? Have fun as you dream big. Be sure to ask the right questions and commit. If your dream is big enough, do the facts count? No.

- List all your wants, then prioritize them. Categorize them in order of importance—a group of "As" (the most important), "Bs" (less important), and "Cs" (least important); then 1 through 10. Goal setting requires serious thought. If it doesn't have more power than your old conditioning, what do you think takes over? Limiting beliefs!

- Take time to reflect on your number one goal.

- Form a clear image of yourself already in possession of your goal and share it with your spouse. Ask him to hold you accountable. Your determination and focus is strengthened when you make a commitment to someone you care about who has your interests at heart.

- Measure your success. Decide what completes the picture, showing that you have reached the destination for this part of your journey. Whatever it is, write your goal from a deep place of gratitude, in the present tense as though it's already in your life. Ensure that you have measurable targets and measurable results. See yourself as the person you choose to be.

When you have finished (although this is never finished—you can add to it always), come together and compare notes. Which areas have similar goals, which are most important to you both? Out of this you can draw up a starting list of goals you both want to achieve together. You can and will still have individual goals too, of course. Discuss your needs and dreams and make a plan. You can see how important this becomes. You can also see how great it will be to know that the dreams that are important to you have a place mapped out in your future together.

FROM MUTUAL PURPOSE, VISION, AND GOALS TO ACTION

A clear, strong purpose combined with vision, goals, and action is the fastest road to success. Are you clear on your purpose and vision? Have you as a couple found something you're so passionate about that you're prepared to do whatever it takes—to overcome obstacles, to be persistent and never give up? To stretch, expand your boundaries and rise to a new level of awareness as you reach the goal posts on the road to your destination?

Growth doesn't just happen. There's a process to follow. First, decide to be true to your purpose and vision; commit to excellence; then practice, practice, practice. Learn and grow; remember what you learned in levels of awareness: you have to acclimatize before moving on to the next level. Expect plateaus and allow for setbacks—they're all part of the rhythm of life.

Second, prepare the plan. What are you going to do to support your purpose and vision? Use your imagination, aided by your senses and emotions, to form a clear, concise image of yourself already having achieved your goal; expect to see it in reality. You don't have to know the "HOW"—the universe takes care of that. You become more inspired as you raise your vibration and start tapping into new ideas and information.

Make a decision, take action, and allow your marriage to happen. Every step you take and every success you celebrate intensifies your resolve and desire to stay strong as a couple.

CHAPTER 8 SUMMARY

- ✓ When couples fall into an "is this all there is" feeling, they lack a shared experience with each other. Couples have to have a mutual purpose, vision, and set of goals. When we visualize our life together, our shared purpose, vision, and goals should always be included. A truly fulfilling marriage begins when a couple comes together and uses their third mind to look through their spouse's eyes and see the same purpose, vision, and goals, which makes it so much more powerful.

- ✓ A purpose-driven marriage gives us a life with intention and direction, and every day that goes by we learn who we are, the meaning of life, and what is truly important for our relationship.

- ✓ If money was no object and there was absolutely no chance of "failure," what would you and your spouse do each day?

- ✓ A successful relationship vision should be aligned with your strengths and core values.

- ✓ Goals grow out of the vision that you and your partner create together. Couples who sit down together DAILY and take the time to spell out what their own expectations, desires, and hopes are have a high chance of future success and happiness together when they make plans for things they both want.

- ✓ A clear, strong purpose combined with vision, goals, and action is the fastest road to a successful and happy marriage.

CHAPTER 8 EXERCISE

Remember the Do's and Don'ts for writing out your mutual vision, purpose, and goals.

1. Do not write down your current needs or do not haves.

   ✓ If you have it all with no restrictions, how do you live your life? This will be your wants (not your needs).

2. The wants is not about how successful your spouse is.

   ✓ It's all about YOU living the life you want in a shared vision / relationship.

3. Do not write about things you do not want in your life and relationship.

   ✓ Write it down in a positive way only (needs examples).

4. Do not let your fears and doubt control your dream; people tend to lower their wants to a reasonable comfortable achievable vision.

   ✓ Your vision is your ideal life. Dare, challenge yourself, use fears as sign that you are in the right direction.

5. Do not think of what your spouse might want for himself or in your mutual dream life.

   ✓ It's all about your wants in your ideal life.

6. Do not let your current circumstances dictate your wants.

   ✓ Think, as you are the ONE in control, you create your own circumstances.

7. Do not list out things: "I want my spouse to do, give, behave, change etc."

   ✓ It's all about YOU, things I want, I love to do, I'm having, etc.

Take a blank piece of paper and a pen and write your mutual vision, purpose, and goals for the relationship with the Do's and Don'ts in mind.

1. Write in the first person (I and we)
2. Write in the present tense.

CHAPTER 9
A DASH OF THIS AND A SPRINKLE OF THAT

"People are lonely because they build walls instead of bridges".

— Joseph F. Newton Men

CHAPTER 9

Have you ever tried to bake a cake without following a recipe? You know the basic ingredients—flour, sugar, eggs. That should be enough, right? Sure, what else goes in a cake? Without another thought, you mix the flour, eggs, and sugar, pour it into a pan, and stick it in the oven. Thirty minutes later, your mouth is watering at the mere sight of the delicious cake. You can't wait to take the first bite. To your dismay, this edible masterpiece looks like a cake but tastes like shit. If you had read the recipe you would have known that vanilla, baking soda, and even salt are all necessary ingredients of a cake.

A healthy marriage is based on five ingredients as well—trust, cooperation, communication, intimacy, and respect. All of these nurture and grow a harmonious relationship. Couples who love one another and experience joy in discovering new things about each other have a strong bond and genuinely enjoy being with each other. If your marriage is missing just one of these ingredients, confusion, doubt, rejection, abandonment, emptiness, anger, sadness, and feelings of betrayal surface. Like the cake we mentioned above, is your relationship really a pile of relationshit? The test of a marriage is a balance between each ingredient. You can communicate every day, but if you don't respect one another than your words are just empty. When a relationship loses the balance of these essential items, chaos moves in and takes over. Let's take a moment and look at each one of these ingredients individually.

TRUST

How is the trust in your relationship? Good? Bad? Not sure? In our work with couples, we often find a lack of trust at the root of many challenges they report. We have been taught to believe trust has to be earned by others. Far too many couples believe that their spouse or partner has to pass certain tests in order to extend their trust. One of the reasons so many couples have issues with trust is that view it in the wrong way. They think of trust in terms of "I trust you not to act in a certain way." For instance, you trust your spouse not to lie or cheat. We believe that you have to trust yourself before you can trust others. In essence, trust is a choice. You can't get from others what you don't possess in yourself. We tell our clients to look at trust from the inside out. Do you trust yourself? Am I a trustworthy person? Does my partner realize that I have integrity and can be trusted? Do I extend trust to them?

Trusting has so much more to do with who you are as a person than it does with who your partner is. When you are secure in yourself and know that you are worthy to receive love, then it trust happens with ease. The law of attraction applies to trust. Since you attract into your life what you focus upon, it makes sense that if you trust yourself you'll attract trust from your partner. If you find that you're constantly disappointed with your spouse because you believe he's lying or acting inappropriately, ask yourself what is it about you that makes you think that way? Remember, you attract what you think about, so take an honest look at yourself to see if you trust who you are. What are your thoughts that actually pull dishonest people into your life? Consequently, if you're happy, open, honest, and comfortable with who you are, more than likely your relationship is built on a solid foundation of mutual trust.

Don't allow a lack of trust in yourself to shake the foundation of your self-confidence. Be the person you want to be in the relationship and soon you'll find your partner acting the way you want her to. We coached a woman who was reluctant to begin a new relationship. She had been divorced for about six years and wanted to meet someone but couldn't get past the first date. She didn't understand why this was happening because she was fun-loving, giving, and attractive. The first question we asked her was if there was something holding her back. She mentioned how she didn't want to hurt anyone again. After a bit more digging, we found out that she was unfaithful in her first marriage and felt tremendous guilt. She didn't trust herself enough to enter into a new relationship because of her past actions. As we continued our discussion, she realized that what really happened is that when she had an affair; it totally shook her self-esteem and belief in herself. If she doesn't like herself, how can someone else be attracted to her?

Trusting yourself allows you to achieve the level of intimacy a trusting relationship provides. Trust yourself as well as your own instincts in people. If you trust in yourself and your good judgment, when you make a mistake you won't be devastated. Remember, we need to trust our partners, but our broader trust should be placed in ourselves.

COOPERATION

Cooperation is the point when you work together to fulfill your mutual vision and goals. For instance, the majority of couples set a goal to raise their children in a certain way.

"When we had children, we agreed that we would always have the same opinion in front of them. If we needed to disagree we would do it behind closed doors, one-on-one."—Ossi

When you and your spouse don't operate from a state of cooperation, you raise resistance. Think about the last time you told your partner that he was wrong and you were right. How did that work out for you? Probably not well. More than likely he resisted your opinion. A couple came to us one time wanting to know why we get along so well. We told them that our relationship is based on love, not arguing. We released all our past grudges against one another and focused on moving forward in love, not backwards in conflict. You need to gain strength from your partner rather than push him away. To do this, however, we have to create a paradigm shift and live from our true beliefs, not those of our parents.

In many marriages, conflict rather than cooperation settles in. Conflict is a habit in our lives. We're in conflict with our jobs, parents, and anything else we don't like. Conflicts sometimes have very long histories. When a couple has regularly given into conflict, it is obvious that they have accepted a destructive way of handling differences. Through our workshops and coaching, we've learned conflict isn't about the argument; it is instead about what you want to gain and ultimately about your self-image. There are millions of reasons for conflict in a relationship, but remember that it is not a real issue, it is just two different perceptions. More than likely, these inclinations to conflict have been passed on for generations. If your parents argued, then you have learned that it is normal to argue. But let us turn this around. Instead of looking at our parents' faults, look at your own marriage. The majority of conflict arises in marriages because of internal conflict. Our reality doesn't match what we feel.

When couples argue they operate from the viewpoint of "I'm right and you're wrong." These perceptions don't matter. In truth, we both see the same thing. We need to take the information from our conflict and devise a new picture of the situation. You have to be able to work together, from the third mind.

Stop for a moment and revisit the last argument you had with your spouse. Did it even make sense? Most of our conflicts are anything but logical reasons presented back and forth—though many of us believe we are right. The problem is quickly aggravated when the other person isn't willing to view the situation from his spouse's eyes. If we can stop for a moment and view the situation through our spouse's eyes, we'll be able to see where she is coming from and what her feelings are. We believe there is no such thing as difference; each of us has something to contribute. Instead of "it's me against you," work together from the thought process of "we're in this together." Most of you could tell us the last two or three things you and your spouse argued about. They are still on your mind because they have hurt you. They are still probably unresolved. This is the way it is with hostilities. Release your past hurts and beliefs and move forward. Even though one person wins the relationship loses.

We worked with one wife who is a great example of this. She and her husband fought constantly over him leaving his clothes on the bathroom floor. She'd yell, "Pick up your clothes! Are your arms broken?" He'd reply, "I'll do it later." Needless to say, the next morning his dirty laundry was still strewn all over the bathroom floor. So she decided to take matters into her own hands. She quit bitching at him, and he thought he won. He may have won the battle but in reality he lost the war. She picked up his clothes and instead of putting them in the laundry basket she simply refolded them and placed them back in his dresser drawers. A couple of weeks later and a lot of complaints from his friends and co-workers, he started to clean up after himself. These troubles go deeper than the actual issue that a couple might argue over. Fortunately, our personal and professional experiences have enabled us to learn a great deal about conflict.

An exercise we use with couples is guided imagery. The next time you get into an argument with your partner imagine that you're having sex and think about the love you have for each other. Hold those thoughts in your mind, and soon they'll replace those of anger and frustration. One woman we coached had a constant conflict with her husband and couldn't understand why. This was her third marriage and his second. She was a successful individual with a strong self-esteem until she came home. The moment she walked in the door she felt vulnerable. So why is it than in her office she felt in control and at home she felt chaos? You see, in her previous marriages her home was not a safe place. She needed to understand the importance of releasing her past thoughts from her previous marriages and move forward with new thoughts for her current marriage. We taught her how to use guided imagery and think happy thoughts when she is at home with her husband. She met with us a week later and told us that she and her husband had the best weekend of their marriage.

Conflict is inevitable, but our reaction to it can be changed. True, we are all unique individuals with distinctive values, opinions and perceptions, but by viewing the relationship through your spouse's eyes, you both can base your relationship on cooperation and love. Cooperation in a marriage makes you and your spouse a team.

COMMUNICATION

Communication is one of the most important ingredients in a relationship. If your spouse is in a good mood, you have good communication, and on the opposite end, if he's in a bad mood, the communication is not so good. Our goal is to have a constant stream of good moods combined with good communication. To do this, you have to have a shift in your thoughts and feelings.

If you were to ask several people the definition of communication, odds are you'll get many different answers. With all the various ideas about communication, how do we know the true meaning of communication? For couples, communication is about listening. We use our ears to hear but not listen. When partners talk to each they hear meanings, not actual words. People attach meanings to what their spouse is saying based on their paradigms. To make matters worse, in most cases, both people are speaking through their paradigms. Paradigms talking to paradigms are like a movie in a foreign language without subtitles. Nobody understands what hell is going on.

Communication in relationships is different from all other forms because when we talk to each other we're inviting someone else into our sacred space. When you invite someone into your sacred space, you believe in them. Belief is a powerful emotion, and your partner can sense it immediately. Listening rather than hearing takes you to a place where you don't have any expectations. Expectations in communication are nothing more than hidden agendas. You want to get something out of the conversation. For instance, you tell your spouse you're tired and had a long day when you really want her to offer to give you a massage. Then when she tells you to go lie down, you get upset because she didn't offer you a back rub. Expectations don't have a place in communication.

"I thought every conversation was meant to get me results. I expected certain things to come from my communication with Osnat. I was wrong, and now that I communicate without expectations and listen, we have a much happier marriage."—Dan

There are two things you never do in communication:

- Give advice.

- React.

Just listen. Have you ever wondered why so many people pray when they have a difficult decision to make or face a crisis? Simple, because God just listens. He doesn't give advice or react in any way. This is what we all want. The answer is already inside of us; we just need someone to listen to us without any expectations. When you truly listen, you're giving back to them, and the relationship is transformed. The best communication happens when you listen because you're able to process information and respond rather than react.

We respond using only our five senses. During communication you need to listen with the following thoughts in mind:

- First understand what the purpose of the discussion not what can you get out of it.

- Next, when you've discovered the purpose, think about what your spouse can gain from the conversation, not how you can benefit.

- Lastly, think about who you are in this conversation. What paradigms are driving you? Are your thoughts really your own or someone else's? Always think about being. By this we mean, are you loving and enthusiastic or short and irritable? Whatever your mood is at the time drives the mood of the conversation.

When we communicate in a relationship we need to also use our intellectual faculties, in particular intuition. Also known as a gut feeling, hunch, or lucky guess, intuition just like communication has many definitions and descriptions. Call it what you want, intuition is a subconscious, specialized source of information that thousands of years ago people understood as a source of protection. In our brains there are two parts; the thinking mind and the feeling mind. The thinking mind works to filter huge amounts of information, blend data, isolate telling details, and come to astonishingly rapid conclusions. Intuition is no different than exercising: in the same manner it takes time to build your body's muscles, it also takes time to build your mental muscles.

The more you practice the better you get at hearing your intuition and knowing what your spouse thinks. A good exercise we use is to sit in front of each other, think of a word or event, stare into each other's eyes, and focus. After a short amount of time, we try to read each other's minds. Just as there is a correlation with exercise and strength there is also one with the success of relationships and intuition. Initially, we couldn't tap into each other's minds, but once we were able to get on same vibration, we were easily able to repeat each other's thoughts. Intuition and the law of vibration are closely linked because every thought you put into the universe vibrates back to you. When you and your spouse create the third mind, you share the same vibration.

Couples who tap into their intuition communicate better because they have the ability to see what each other wants before the other person even asks. When we're in tune with our intuition, we have more opportunities for good relationships because intuition and right brain functioning add creativity, humor, and the ability to solve problems, to reach goals, and to communicate more effectively. In a marriage, feelings and emotions are at the base of communication, so it makes sense that if we can tap into each other's feelings through intuition that the relationship benefits. Everyone has intuition; it is just a matter of learning to listen to it.

Stop for a moment and think about the times you had a strong feeling about your spouse when they called you on the phone or walked in the door. Has there ever been a time when you just knew that they were going to come home with some good news to tell you? Based on this instinct, you approached them in a positive manner. How were your results? In all reality, your instinctive actions helped to make a happy situation even more exciting. We all have flashes of intuition, but many of us ignore or distrust them as irrational and useless distractions.

If we learn to listen deeply enough, intuition reveals significant, profound insight into the feelings, thoughts, and emotions of our partner. Couples are most influenced by what they feel rather than the words they hear. The majority of us act from 80 percent emotion and 20 percent logic. Imagine how much better your relationship would be if you trained yourself to tap into your partner's feelings and have them do the same? Intuition is real and innate in all of us. We all have a certain intuition, and the longer we're in the relationship, the stronger it becomes and the more we trust ourselves to use it. A good way to start is to ask yourself, does it smell right, feel right, fit right?

Intuition has and continues to play a part in the success of our marriage. Intuition gives us the ability to determine our partner's wants and needs before he even speaks. Why is this so important? Simple, because it gives you the knowledge needed to respond rather than react.

If you truly want to forge a lasting relationship, you need to become more conscious of your intuitive faculty and practice it with your spouse. Intuition can do much more for you than help you find out what your spouse wants. It can also help you integrate those answers so that you can use them to change your attitude and actions toward him. Intuition allows you to make the right decision quickly, even without all the facts.

Intuitive messages come in numbers of ways. They can come when you experience a hunch, realistic dream, vision, or a very strong feeling. They can also be expressed through the body, such as tightness in your chest, a distinct change in energy, or an overwhelming surge of emotions. Because so many of today's relationships, depending upon the situation, are often chaotic, rational forms of decision-making are difficult, especially when heightened emotions are involved; we need to be able to fall back on our intuition. As couples begin to implement intuition into their communication, they uncover and actualize the limitless potential of their relationship.

INTIMACY

Intimacy is where sex meets romance. It is when you let your spouse into your sacred space and enjoy it. True intimacy occurs between you and your partner when you both have reached the highest level of awareness—mastery. Intimacy opens spiritual and emotional doors where you get to know each other in a deep way. Intimacy in relationships is fundamental for both parties to feel fulfilled. Most people look for intimacy but don't know how to find it. When we create the third mind, we've connected to the deepest sense of intimacy. To do this, you have to release all of your old beliefs and hurts. Reevaluate your thoughts and behaviors and find out if they are your own. It is those factors that draw you far from your spouse that cause lack of intimacy.

Intimacy is not just sex. Yes, that is a good benefit, but what we want more is emotional intimacy. We like to tell people to have sex through the eyes first and then through the body. When you see each other in their true light you're able to understand each other's feelings, which leads to great physical intimacy and trust. This is a deep connection with your spouse and occurs when each person is completely open-hearted and devoted to taking 100 percent responsibility for their own feelings and needs. It occurs when each person is deeply connected with his or her own true self. When people are living with their own thoughts they're able to make an inner connection and share love with others. Out of intimacy comes fun, learning, growth, and creativity.

True intimacy in a relationship comes from a deep commitment to rid yourself of your paradigms and the ability to trust yourself. Emotional intimacy also stems from intuition. It is the natural outgrowth of developing intuition with ourselves and our spouse. The more inner work we do to heal the fears and beliefs that limit us and learn to be open and honest with ourselves, the more open and authentic we will be in our relationship. Through the daily practice of learning to take full responsibility for our own feelings and needs, we are more able to give love to our spouse and to contribute to the relationship.

RESPECT

Respect is the same as trust in the sense that if you don't respect yourself you can't respect others. How do you think about yourself? Do you feel worthy of love? No one else can respect you if you don't respect yourself. In our home country of Israel we were taught that you have to work hard to gain respect, but we disagree. We think it's not about work at all. Instead, you have to have a good self-image and respect yourself for others to do the same. Think back to the law of vibration—our thoughts emit a certain vibration, and others are able to read it. What type of energy are you emitting? Whatever you think about yourself is what other people see and feel.

When a person comes to us with a negative feeling, we initially tell them to change their language. Our minds can't process a negative, so if someone tells you "don't be afraid," what happens is that you're afraid. Why? Because you're focusing on the fear. Instead, change your language. Next, we give them an exercise. Let's say, for example, the fear of failure is causing one of our clients to lose respect for himself. We first ask him where he feels this fear—chest, head, or back? Then we tell him to give it a color and shape. One of our clients, for example, made one of his fears a round ball and black. Next, imagine the object and think of a tool such as a pair of pliers or shovel to remove it. Then, close your eyes and imagine the tool actually removing it from your body. In the case of our client, he imagined removing a black, round object from his chest with a pair of pliers. This allows the visual of actually removing it from the physical body. This is so important because the mind needs to know for certain that it has been removed. Your mind can't bury something that has been removed.

We then ask what your body feel like without the object—lighter, happier, less anxious? When we get our answer, we then tell clients to take the object and throw it as far into outer space as they can. In the final stage of this exercise, we tell our clients to find a new positive something to put into the vacant space. Again, we ask them to give a shape and color. Our client chose confidence and gave it a red, flat shape. In the final stage of this exercise, we tell them to breathe in and fill the void with the new shape and color. Doing this everyday helps to replace a negative thought and feeling with a positive one that moves them forward. Once we eliminate the negative thoughts in our lives and focus on the positive, we enter a mindset of respect. This mindset then allows us to become grateful, humble, and well-adjusted, which in turn improves our relationship. When we have self-respect, we love ourselves and are able to love others.

A fulfilled marriage isn't just about love and sex like so many think. Trust, cooperation, communication, intimacy, and respect are important ingredients to any relationship. They all need to be in place equally. For example, building trust in relationships comes from having honest open communication at all times. Also, your self-image can't be based on the opinion of your partner; you need to respect yourself before you're able to find intimacy. Communication allows you to talk to your partner about anything and everything, which fosters cooperation rather than conflict. One ingredient is dependent on another. When all five ingredients actively work together, your relationship is much like a delicious cake. You want more.

CHAPTER 9 SUMMARY

- ✓ A healthy marriage is based on five ingredients—trust, cooperation, communication, intimacy, and respect.
- ✓ Trusting has so much more to do with who we are as a person than it does with who our partner is.
- ✓ Trust allows us to achieve the level of intimacy a trusting relationship provides.
- ✓ When couples argue, they operate from the viewpoint of "I'm right and you're wrong."
- ✓ Conflict is inevitable, but by viewing the relationship through our spouse's eyes, we both can base our relationship on cooperation and love.
- ✓ For couples, communication is about listening. We use our ears to hear but not to listen.
- ✓ Communication in relationships is different from all other forms because when we talk to each other we're inviting someone else into our sacred space.
- ✓ Intimacy is where sex meets romance.
- ✓ Intimacy opens spiritual and emotional doors where you get to know each other in a deep way.
- ✓ Through the daily practice of learning to take full responsibility for our own feelings and needs, we are more able to respect our spouse and contribute to the relationship.
- ✓ No one else can respect us if we don't respect ourselves.

CHAPTER 9 EXERCISE

Select one or more of the ingredient that you feel are missing in your relationship.

What are the outcomes that you want to achieve by improving or adding this ingredient to your relationship?

Write three things that can prevent you from executing these actions.

Write three things that will help you to achieve the results that you want.

CHAPTER 10
A NEW REALITY

"You know you're in love when you can't fall asleep because reality is finally better than your dreams".

–Dr. Seuss

CHAPTER 10

Sometimes couples come to us thinking that a good relationship is nothing more than the ability to know what their spouse thinks or wants before they say anything. In a good relationship you never have to guess what the other person is thinking. Doing so only leads the relationship down a hole of confusion, conflict, and misunderstanding. If, for instance, you presume that your husband wants to be hugged and kissed after he comes in the door from work and all he really wants is to be left alone, were do you think it will get you?

Everyone wants to have a crystal ball so they can look into the future, but the future is not in the ball. It instead lies in each of us. If we can clearly decide what we want and draw it in picture we can create our own future. Why then for God's sake are people still looking for their future in a crystal ball? When people spend their time looking into crystal balls or asking fortune tellers about what the future holds for them what they don't realize is that the future they so desperately want to find out about is a picture chosen by others. Instead, why not gather all your puzzle pieces and create your own picture.

> *"Once I met a friend who told me about an astrologist and numerologist that told her lots of stuff about her future, and she suggested I should go. I told her that I do not want to let anyone to tell me my future, I want to create my own."*

In the previous chapters we talked about beliefs and habits (paradigms), which most of the time are not even yours. After reading the previous chapters and completing the exercises you should by now have all the tools you need to choose your own habits and beliefs, stop imitating others, take control of your life, and have the best relationship possible.

All we have to do is to use our imagination, hold our thoughts, and truly believe and our goals become reality. The problem with most couples today is that they're living according to their parents' paradigms and they don't see themselves for who they truly are. We are the creators of our future, which is why it is so important to be careful what we think.

We first need to determine what level of awareness we're living in. Do you react rather than respond? (Animal) Does your marriage suffer conflict because you compare it with your parents' or friends'? (Mass) Next, we have to accept responsibility for our life to feel empowered and to love and accept ourselves before we can expect our partner to. Honor how you feel and your spouse will soon do the same. We have to change our thinking and release the past. Think consciously, allow "what is," and acknowledge it; then let go and you'll be able to discover who you are and where you're heading in life together. Decide on a mutual purpose, create your vision, set goals, and take action, which then gives you the power to be, do, and have the relationship you choose.

FEELINGS VS. EMOTION

Our life is really an ocean of emotion (sea of love at best). If we ask people what they really want, most people will say they want to live in joy. This is true, but the only way to live in a harmonic relationship is to combine the waves (positive vibrations) of the ocean with our emotions (positive feelings). Once we combine the two we can then create joy.

Let's say for a moment that we do have a crystal ball, and we are looking in to it to find our ideal relationship, the one that we really want. This is our magic ball, it's shows us an alternative future and a glimpse into our ideal life. But soon the ball cracks, and we can no longer see into the ball. So now it is time to look for an alternative way to find our reality. Even better than a crystal ball are your spouse's eyes. As they are your crystal ball, transmit your positive feelings and get the picture of your dream through his eyes.

Remember, our thoughts and feelings have brought us here. New thoughts and feelings will take us from a relationshit to a relationship. We cannot live our life through anger, disappointment, etc. and expect for things to change. Everything starts with imagination. In order to create your ultimate relationship you need to imagine it first, or if you'd like, imagine a crystal ball.

How you feel hugely impacts what you attract into your life. Before continuing, it's important to distinguish this difference between feelings and emotions. Both represent different aspects of the same experience. There's a connection; like so much in life, everything is connected, but there is also a subtle difference.

Feelings represent the physical awareness of an experience; what sensation you feel in your body when you react to what you're experiencing or thinking. They arise from either internal or external stimulation. They might bubble up from within and cause a tingling in your stomach, for example, or you might react to what you're experiencing externally through your senses—to what you're seeing, hearing, smelling, tasting, or touching—and that triggers a response—a feeling based on past experiences, those memories stored in your subconscious mind.

Emotions, on the other hand, are the "psychological state of being" resulting from your thoughts and experiences—how your body reacts to them. In other words, your feelings give rise to your emotions. As you think about and observe your feelings, you become a certain way. Concentrating on happy thoughts puts your relationship in a state of happiness.

When you choose to feel happy and at peace in the present moment, the only moment—now—despite what's going on in the world around you or in your personal circumstances, you have instructed the universe to give you more of the same, and what could be better? To move forward though, there's work to be done and actions to be taken. It's not enough to just feel great. Life happens. How can you feel great about your partner if you don't love and accept yourself; or if you're drifting through life aimlessly; or if you've suffered so much throughout your relationship?

Our level of awareness is critical because most people instinctively think their life circumstances cause their feelings, but in actuality they just provide a stimulus. Your beliefs determine how you feel; and how you feel activates the law of attraction. We have to acknowledge our feelings and respect them. They're real and you can't change anything you don't acknowledge. Everyone reacts differently based on their beliefs and personality. There's no right or wrong—it "just is."

In "levels of awareness" we learned that it's a gradual jump from one level to another. It's the same with our relationship. To go from the lowest emotion to the highest—from depression to joy—in one leap is far too much for the mind to accept. Again, we acclimatize to a better-feeling emotion by choosing a better-feeling thought, thereby attracting the same from our spouse. And the better we get, the better they get. A relationship is never smooth sailing, and if it is you may even feel bored after a while! Everyone faces adversity at some point—it's how you handle it that counts. Do you feel sorry for yourself, focusing on what's missing from your life? Or are you grateful for all the positives that emerge? The difference between the resilient relationships and those who remain stuck boils down to attitude. When your relationship becomes stagnate, take action. Talk to your spouse or partner about your experience. Remove any emotional attachment to the experience. It will always remain a part of your life, and so it should—it's shaped you into the person you are today. However, remember that you have the power to change by releasing old beliefs and feelings.

FORGIVENESS

Forgiveness is a critical step you need to learn to release and move forward. We'd like to point out that forgiveness doesn't mean you're condoning a certain type of behavior; instead it means you're letting go of all suffering, pain, guilt, or blame from the past. To forgive comes from the heart, otherwise it is not forgiveness. Saying I'm sorry is not really forgiveness. The purpose of forgiveness is not to forget; it's to explore the feeling your truth has created and to understand it and release. Forgive and accept yourself for who you are, a person who is trying to live. Then, and only then, can you move forward in life.

When your relationship isn't working as you'd like there's usually resistance—something you're holding on to from the past: regret, guilt, shame, hurt, anger, or perhaps judgment. Forgiveness is an act of faith. To truly forgive is to be able to embrace your spouse, look her in the eye, and feel her feelings. We discovered that in our marriage it is not about "getting rid of" the painful feelings but rather about embracing them and "transmuting" them to a higher vibration. Basic physics tells us that energy cannot be eliminated—only transformed—and forgiveness accomplishes this.

The main problem when couples forgive each other is through their language. The words "I forgive you" make you superior to your partner, which gives him low self-esteem. Forgiveness is not about right or wrong. To forgive and move forward, we have to make a decision to release unwanted feelings now. The key to healing is to love yourself and others unconditionally and to be willing to forgive—and that includes yourself. Stop standing in judgment of what you've achieved or haven't achieved; of how you look compared to how you'd like to look. Stop putting yourself down—what are you thinking! How does that make you feel? Yes, you may have made "mistakes" in the past, but hasn't everyone? And aren't you here to learn the lessons and to grow and evolve into the best person you can be? There's a rhythm to life, and everything is equal and opposite—by law. Forgive yourself and your spouse from the heart, not the head, and move forward in life.

We have to release any resentment, blame, or guilt in our relationship. If you're jealous or resentful of your spouse because she makes more money than you, you'll stay in the same situation! Why? Because the negative energy in the emotions of jealousy and resentment highlights your own lack a high paying career. Your focus is on what you don't have by being jealous of someone who has it, and as a result you move away from what you desire. You're broadcasting negativity to the universe, and that's what you attract. Instead, support your spouse, and in so doing you support yourself. What you give out comes back to you, multiplied.

By loving and forgiving yourself now you also give yourself permission to love and forgive others, despite what they've done to you. You can't undo the past, but you can say sorry and move forward. Below is an exercise to help you and your partner forgive each other of some longstanding resentment or hurt.

Enter into a relaxed state. Invite your spouse to come and join you in your sacred place. Appreciate his humanness. Allow your inner self to speak. Listen to what really happened between you and your mate; you are forgiving because your story has probably changed dramatically as you've replayed it time and time again. You may have suppressed some things; you may have magnified others. Does your partner have anything to say from his heart? Ask him to speak from his soul; to pour out his heart so you understand the situation from another perspective.

Once you've seen his side of the story, look at the situation through his eyes and release. Visualize the pain, suffering, or guilt leaving your body—you may even see a color. Feel the feelings of relief and hear the sounds as the negative energy dissipates. Notice how your body feels right now as you forgive and release and as you send love to all those sharing this experience with you. For as you heal yourself you also heal others. As you love yourself, you also love others, and as you forgive yourself, you also forgive others. Everything and everyone is connected as one. What did you just learn about yourself? What does your life look like now that you've released and forgiven yourself or those who have caused pain and suffering in your life?

GRATITUDE

To appreciate yourself and others, to love and accept yourself is pure joy. Gratitude is one of the highest of vibrations. The more time you spend appreciating things in your life rather than trying to fix them, the easier it will become to maintain that higher frequency. When you're asking for guidance or for help—which is what prayer is—imagine and feel that you already have it. See it, feel it, and be grateful to the universe in advance because in your mind you already do have it. Come from a place of appreciation and gratitude rather than from a place of wanting. Feel gratitude from the heart. The law of attraction responds to the feelings of appreciation and gratitude, to the emotion attached to the words you use, feeling the language of the subconscious mind. It's the energy—the vibration—of your feelings that the universe responds to.

At first when we wrote our goals we would read them every morning, doing our best to imagine already having them and being grateful, but we had difficulty feeling the excitement and gratitude. Nothing manifested for us in the way we intended until we understood the importance of feelings and emotions. To speak words is one thing but to feel them is another.

It's not what you say that counts; it's what you do. It's the acts of kindness; the appreciation for "what is"; the joy in the simple things—there's so much to be grateful for, and when you realize this and truly live with an "attitude of gratitude," you become unstoppable. You're safe; you're connected; you radiate love.

Look around you. What are you grateful for? No matter how much pain you're experiencing or how dire your circumstances, you'll be surprised at the gifts waiting to be acknowledged. Sort for them—direct your internal filters to all that's good and bring more of that into your life. Who wants to notice the not so good and attract more of that? It's your life at stake here; make the most of every opportunity—it may be a long, long time before you're back!

When you find yourself facing difficult times, ask: "What can I learn from this in order to create a better life from now on? How does this serve me?"

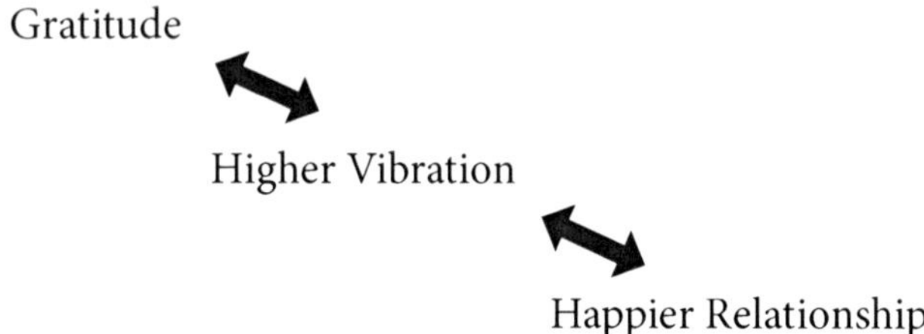

We suggest you keep a gratitude journal. This could be anything from an ordinary notebook to a pad with a pretty cover that pleases you to a formal journal. Writing is an excellent way of staying on a positive wavelength. When you feel love, appreciation, and gratitude your heart rhythm is coherent rather than chaotic. In your journal write down everything you can think of that gives you joy and a feeling of gratitude—big things, little things, anything! It can be something that's already happened or something you're expecting to happen—the subconscious mind doesn't know the difference between real and imagined.

Why not start your day by appreciating in advance what you're grateful for—you already have it in your "mind's eye." Then at the end of the day record everything that happened for which you're grateful—everything. This instructs your subconscious mind to focus on what's good in your life and to bring you more.

It's easy to be grateful when you look at what's really important in life; it can be such simple things that make the difference. When you really start to think about it, there's so much to appreciate and be grateful for. Go about your day saying "thank you" for all that you have or are about to have. As you write in your gratitude journal, notice how you feel. When you're focused on the good in life you raise your vibration.

LIVE IN THE NOW

To love someone unconditionally, without trying to change them, is to truly give love; to focus on their strengths, not their weaknesses; to trust your loved ones can handle their life themselves, and to let go! This has been a huge lesson for us and as we embrace it, we feel a sense of freedom. Love is vital for your happiness and healthy survival. In the past most of us have searched for love externally rather than looking within. A lack of knowledge of universal laws led us to believe that we were being unfairly treated when life didn't happen according to plan. Yet in reality our experiences are always perfect for our growth.

Love is always present, waiting to be taken by the hand; waiting for us to recognize that we are all evolving at different rates and operating at different levels; waiting for us to remember that we are all part of the same puzzle, that we are connected. Love is the ultimate energy—it's all there is. All else is merely an illusion, even fear, it's opposite. Fearful thoughts produce fearful results; loving thoughts produce loving results.

When you feel the love within, it's natural to project it outwards. People feel your loving energy. They're attracted to you. They respond to your kind words and actions, whether it's a simple smile of acknowledgement or something on a grand scale. It's the love behind the action that's so powerful. Kindness spreads. Encouragement empowers. When you live from an inner core of love, fear dissolves. It cannot survive.

Stop feeling guilty over things you'd rather not have done in the past or reliving painful experiences over and over again, each time embellishing them and sinking further into victimhood. You know that releasing transmutes suffering into peace. And you know that there is only one moment in time that's real—now, not the past, not the future, but now—so it's time to pay attention to this truth and to withdraw your focus from the past and future whenever these two "illusions of time" are not required. Both the past and the future are figments of your imagination.

What's the point of thinking about freedom in the future? Think about freedom now. Grow into the person you are becoming now. See yourself as the "New You" and remember that how you're vibrating in the present moment activates the law of attraction. It responds to how you're feeling now. Imagine living this way, feeling truly alive. Imagine being able to release negative emotions as they arise, knowing that they're more than likely a response to beliefs that were formed when you were a child. Imagine feeling free and at peace within— now! Does that sound great? Guess what—this could be your life if you pay attention to it!

"I'll be happy when we move to a bigger house"; "I'll be happy when we have children"; "I'll be happy when we stop arguing"; or "I'll be happy when we feel financially secure." Do these sentiments seem familiar? Have you ever found that when you finally do achieve these things, the joy is only momentary? So many people misunderstand how life flows. They believe that when they have what they want they'll behave and feel differently. They come from the perspective of "having first, then doing, and finally being or feeling a certain way," yet it works the other way around. External experiences or possessions rarely bring you lasting happiness—it's only temporary. Look within and change within—that's where you find true happiness.

Adopt a new approach: "be" first, then "do," and you'll finally "have" your desire. Everything that's happened in life happened in a former; and everything that happens in the future is an imagined; how do you create the future you want? The future lies in each of us; we need to living in the present moment—now!

CHAPTER 10 SUMMARY

- ✓ Most couples live according to their parents' paradigms, and they don't see themselves for who they truly are.

- ✓ We are the creators of our future, which is why it is so important to be careful what we think.

- ✓ Feelings represent the physical awareness of an experience; what sensation we feel in our body when we react to what we're experiencing or thinking.

- ✓ Emotions are the "psychological state of being" resulting from our thoughts and experiences—how our body reacts to them.

- ✓ Concentrating on happy thoughts puts us and our relationship in a state of happiness.

CHAPTER 10 EXERCISE

Look into your partner's eyes each time you need to know what the future holds for your relationship. Practice seeing your relationship through the third mind to create a new reality.

CPSIA information can be obtained at www.ICGtesting.com
Printed in the USA
244755LV00002B/1/P

9 781599 303987